PHONE CALL

LOG BOOK

NAME:

_____

COMPANY:

_____

_____

ADDRESS:

_____

_____

PHONE:

_____

EMAIL:

_____

_____

Your purchase of the Phone Call Log Book from us is greatly appreciated. We are working hard to build even better products for you. We would love to hear your thoughts and opinions. Please don't hesitate to contact us with your comments or suggestions.

Thank you!

📅 Date: _____ **🕐 Time:** _____

  Caller: _____

🏢 Company: _____

📞 Phone: _____

📧 Email: _____

☼ Urgency: ☐ Low ☐ Medium ☐ High

💬 Message: _____

📞 Called ☐

📅 Date: _____ **🕐 Time:** _____

📞 Caller: _____

🏢 Company: _____

📞 Phone: _____

@ Email: _____

☼ Urgency: ☐ Low ☐ Medium ☐ High

💬 Message: _____

📞 Called ☐

📅 Date: _____ **🕐 Time:** _____

📞 Caller: _____

🏢 Company: _____

📞 Phone: _____

@ Email: _____

☼ Urgency: ☐ Low ☐ Medium ☐ High

💬 Message: _____

📞 Called ☐

📅 Date: _____ **🕐 Time:** _____

📞 Caller: _____

🏢 Company: _____

📞 Phone: _____

@ Email: _____

☼ Urgency: ☐ Low ☐ Medium ☐ High

💬 Message: _____

📞 Called ☐

📅 Date: _____ **🕐 Time:** _____

📞 Caller: _____

🏢 Company: _____

📞 Phone: _____

@ Email: _____

☼ Urgency: ☐ Low ☐ Medium ☐ High

💬 Message: _____

📞 Called ☐

🗓 Date:	🕐 Time:	💬 Message:
👤 Caller:		
🏢 Company:		
📞 Phone:		
@ Email:		
☀ Urgency: ☐ Low ☐ Medium ☐ High		📞 Called ☐

🗓 Date:	🕐 Time:	💬 Message:
👤 Caller:		
🏢 Company:		
📞 Phone:		
@ Email:		
☀ Urgency: ☐ Low ☐ Medium ☐ High		📞 Called ☐

🗓 Date:	🕐 Time:	💬 Message:
👤 Caller:		
🏢 Company:		
📞 Phone:		
@ Email:		
☀ Urgency: ☐ Low ☐ Medium ☐ High		📞 Called ☐

🗓 Date:	🕐 Time:	💬 Message:
👤 Caller:		
🏢 Company:		
📞 Phone:		
@ Email:		
☀ Urgency: ☐ Low ☐ Medium ☐ High		📞 Called ☐

🗓 Date:	🕐 Time:	💬 Message:
👤 Caller:		
🏢 Company:		
📞 Phone:		
@ Email:		
☀ Urgency: ☐ Low ☐ Medium ☐ High		📞 Called ☐

Date: **Time:**   **Message:**

Caller:

Company:

Phone:

Email:

Urgency: ☐ Low   ☐ Medium   ☐ High   **Called** ☐

Date: **Time:**   **Message:**

Caller:

Company:

Phone:

Email:

Urgency: ☐ Low   ☐ Medium   ☐ High   **Called** ☐

Date: **Time:**   **Message:**

Caller:

Company:

Phone:

Email:

Urgency: ☐ Low   ☐ Medium   ☐ High   **Called** ☐

Date: **Time:**   **Message:**

Caller:

Company:

Phone:

Email:

Urgency: ☐ Low   ☐ Medium   ☐ High   **Called** ☐

Date: **Time:**   **Message:**

Caller:

Company:

Phone:

Email:

Urgency: ☐ Low   ☐ Medium   ☐ High   **Called** ☐

🗓 Date:	🕐 Time:	💬 Message:
👥 Caller:		
🏢 Company:		
📞 Phone:		
@ Email:		
🔔 Urgency: ☐ Low ☐ Medium ☐ High		📞 Called ☐

🗓 Date:	🕐 Time:	💬 Message:
👥 Caller:		
🏢 Company:		
📞 Phone:		
@ Email:		
🔔 Urgency: ☐ Low ☐ Medium ☐ High		📞 Called ☐

🗓 Date:	🕐 Time:	💬 Message:
👥 Caller:		
🏢 Company:		
📞 Phone:		
@ Email:		
🔔 Urgency: ☐ Low ☐ Medium ☐ High		📞 Called ☐

🗓 Date:	🕐 Time:	💬 Message:
👥 Caller:		
🏢 Company:		
📞 Phone:		
@ Email:		
🔔 Urgency: ☐ Low ☐ Medium ☐ High		📞 Called ☐

🗓 Date:	🕐 Time:	💬 Message:
👥 Caller:		
🏢 Company:		
📞 Phone:		
@ Email:		
🔔 Urgency: ☐ Low ☐ Medium ☐ High		📞 Called ☐

📅 Date:	🕐 Time:	💬 Message:
Caller:		
🏢 Company:		
📞 Phone:		
📧 Email:		
☼ Urgency: ☐ Low ☐ Medium ☐ High		📞 Called ☐

📅 Date:	🕐 Time:	💬 Message:
👤 Caller:		
🏢 Company:		
📞 Phone:		
@ Email:		
☼ Urgency: ☐ Low ☐ Medium ☐ High		📞 Called ☐

📅 Date:	🕐 Time:	💬 Message:
👤 Caller:		
🏢 Company:		
📞 Phone:		
@ Email:		
☼ Urgency: ☐ Low ☐ Medium ☐ High		📞 Called ☐

📅 Date:	🕐 Time:	💬 Message:
👤 Caller:		
🏢 Company:		
📞 Phone:		
@ Email:		
☼ Urgency: ☐ Low ☐ Medium ☐ High		📞 Called ☐

📅 Date:	🕐 Time:	💬 Message:
👤 Caller:		
🏢 Company:		
📞 Phone:		
@ Email:		
☼ Urgency: ☐ Low ☐ Medium ☐ High		📞 Called ☐

🗓 Date:	🕐 Time:	💬 Message:
👥 Caller:		
🏢 Company:		
📞 Phone:		
@ Email:		
🚨 Urgency: ☐ Low ☐ Medium ☐ High		📞 Called ☐

🗓 Date:	🕐 Time:	💬 Message:
👥 Caller:		
🏢 Company:		
📞 Phone:		
@ Email:		
🚨 Urgency: ☐ Low ☐ Medium ☐ High		📞 Called ☐

🗓 Date:	🕐 Time:	💬 Message:
👥 Caller:		
🏢 Company:		
📞 Phone:		
@ Email:		
🚨 Urgency: ☐ Low ☐ Medium ☐ High		📞 Called ☐

🗓 Date:	🕐 Time:	💬 Message:
👥 Caller:		
🏢 Company:		
📞 Phone:		
@ Email:		
🚨 Urgency: ☐ Low ☐ Medium ☐ High		📞 Called ☐

🗓 Date:	🕐 Time:	💬 Message:
👥 Caller:		
🏢 Company:		
📞 Phone:		
@ Email:		
🚨 Urgency: ☐ Low ☐ Medium ☐ High		📞 Called ☐

✉ Date: ⏰ Time: 💬 Message:

👤 Caller:

🏢 Company:

📞 Phone:

📧 Email:

🔆 Urgency: ☐ Low ☐ Medium ☐ High   📞 Called ☐

✉ Date: ⏰ Time: 💬 Message:

👤 Caller:

🏢 Company:

📞 Phone:

@ Email:

🔆 Urgency: ☐ Low ☐ Medium ☐ High   📞 Called ☐

✉ Date: ⏰ Time: 💬 Message:

👤 Caller:

🏢 Company:

📞 Phone:

@ Email:

🔆 Urgency: ☐ Low ☐ Medium ☐ High   📞 Called ☐

✉ Date: ⏰ Time: 💬 Message:

👤 Caller:

🏢 Company:

📞 Phone:

@ Email:

🔆 Urgency: ☐ Low ☐ Medium ☐ High   📞 Called ☐

✉ Date: ⏰ Time: 💬 Message:

👤 Caller:

🏢 Company:

📞 Phone:

@ Email:

🔆 Urgency: ☐ Low ☐ Medium ☐ High   📞 Called ☐

📅 Date:	🕐 Time:	💬 Message:
👤 Caller:		
🏢 Company:		
📞 Phone:		
@ Email:		
🔆 Urgency: ☐ Low ☐ Medium ☐ High		📞 Called ☐

📅 Date:	🕐 Time:	💬 Message:
👤 Caller:		
🏢 Company:		
📞 Phone:		
@ Email:		
🔆 Urgency: ☐ Low ☐ Medium ☐ High		📞 Called ☐

📅 Date:	🕐 Time:	💬 Message:
👤 Caller:		
🏢 Company:		
📞 Phone:		
@ Email:		
🔆 Urgency: ☐ Low ☐ Medium ☐ High		📞 Called ☐

📅 Date:	🕐 Time:	💬 Message:
👤 Caller:		
🏢 Company:		
📞 Phone:		
@ Email:		
🔆 Urgency: ☐ Low ☐ Medium ☐ High		📞 Called ☐

📅 Date:	🕐 Time:	💬 Message:
👤 Caller:		
🏢 Company:		
📞 Phone:		
@ Email:		
🔆 Urgency: ☐ Low ☐ Medium ☐ High		📞 Called ☐

Date: **Time:**

Caller:

Company:

Phone:

Email:

Urgency: ☐ Low   ☐ Medium   ☐ High

Message:

Called ☐

Date: **Time:**

Caller:

Company:

Phone:

Email:

Urgency: ☐ Low   ☐ Medium   ☐ High

Message:

Called ☐

Date: **Time:**

Caller:

Company:

Phone:

Email:

Urgency: ☐ Low   ☐ Medium   ☐ High

Message:

Called ☐

Date: **Time:**

Caller:

Company:

Phone:

Email:

Urgency: ☐ Low   ☐ Medium   ☐ High

Message:

Called ☐

Date: **Time:**

Caller:

Company:

Phone:

Email:

Urgency: ☐ Low   ☐ Medium   ☐ High

Message:

Called ☐

📷 Date:	🕐 Time:	💬 Message:
👤 Caller:		
🏢 Company:		
📞 Phone:		
@ Email:		
☀ Urgency: ☐ Low ☐ Medium ☐ High		📞 Called ☐

📷 Date:	🕐 Time:	💬 Message:
👤 Caller:		
🏢 Company:		
📞 Phone:		
@ Email:		
☀ Urgency: ☐ Low ☐ Medium ☐ High		📞 Called ☐

📷 Date:	🕐 Time:	💬 Message:
👤 Caller:		
🏢 Company:		
📞 Phone:		
@ Email:		
☀ Urgency: ☐ Low ☐ Medium ☐ High		📞 Called ☐

📷 Date:	🕐 Time:	💬 Message:
👤 Caller:		
🏢 Company:		
📞 Phone:		
@ Email:		
☀ Urgency: ☐ Low ☐ Medium ☐ High		📞 Called ☐

📷 Date:	🕐 Time:	💬 Message:
👤 Caller:		
🏢 Company:		
📞 Phone:		
@ Email:		
☀ Urgency: ☐ Low ☐ Medium ☐ High		📞 Called ☐

📅 Date:	🕐 Time:	💬 Message:
👤 Caller:		
🏢 Company:		
📞 Phone:		
@ Email:		
🔆 Urgency: ☐ Low ☐ Medium ☐ High		📞 Called ☐

📅 Date:	🕐 Time:	💬 Message:
👤 Caller:		
🏢 Company:		
📞 Phone:		
@ Email:		
🔆 Urgency: ☐ Low ☐ Medium ☐ High		📞 Called ☐

📅 Date:	🕐 Time:	💬 Message:
👤 Caller:		
🏢 Company:		
📞 Phone:		
@ Email:		
🔆 Urgency: ☐ Low ☐ Medium ☐ High		📞 Called ☐

📅 Date:	🕐 Time:	💬 Message:
👤 Caller:		
🏢 Company:		
📞 Phone:		
@ Email:		
🔆 Urgency: ☐ Low ☐ Medium ☐ High		📞 Called ☐

📅 Date:	🕐 Time:	💬 Message:
👤 Caller:		
🏢 Company:		
📞 Phone:		
@ Email:		
🔆 Urgency: ☐ Low ☐ Medium ☐ High		📞 Called ☐

📇 Date:	🕐 Time:
👤 Caller:	
🏢 Company:	
📞 Phone:	
@ Email:	
🔔 Urgency: ☐ Low ☐ Medium ☐ High	

💬 Message:

📞 Called ☐

📇 Date:	🕐 Time:
👤 Caller:	
🏢 Company:	
📞 Phone:	
@ Email:	
🔔 Urgency: ☐ Low ☐ Medium ☐ High	

💬 Message:

📞 Called ☐

📇 Date:	🕐 Time:
👤 Caller:	
🏢 Company:	
📞 Phone:	
@ Email:	
🔔 Urgency: ☐ Low ☐ Medium ☐ High	

💬 Message:

📞 Called ☐

📇 Date:	🕐 Time:
👤 Caller:	
🏢 Company:	
📞 Phone:	
@ Email:	
🔔 Urgency: ☐ Low ☐ Medium ☐ High	

💬 Message:

📞 Called ☐

📇 Date:	🕐 Time:
👤 Caller:	
🏢 Company:	
📞 Phone:	
@ Email:	
🔔 Urgency: ☐ Low ☐ Medium ☐ High	

💬 Message:

📞 Called ☐

Entry 1

Date: _____ **Time:** _____

Caller: _____

Company: _____

Phone: _____

Email: _____

Urgency: ☐ Low ☐ Medium ☐ High

Message:

Called ☐

Entry 2

Date: _____ **Time:** _____

Caller: _____

Company: _____

Phone: _____

Email: _____

Urgency: ☐ Low ☐ Medium ☐ High

Message:

Called ☐

Entry 3

Date: _____ **Time:** _____

Caller: _____

Company: _____

Phone: _____

Email: _____

Urgency: ☐ Low ☐ Medium ☐ High

Message:

Called ☐

Entry 4

Date: _____ **Time:** _____

Caller: _____

Company: _____

Phone: _____

Email: _____

Urgency: ☐ Low ☐ Medium ☐ High

Message:

Called ☐

Entry 5

Date: _____ **Time:** _____

Caller: _____

Company: _____

Phone: _____

Email: _____

Urgency: ☐ Low ☐ Medium ☐ High

Message:

Called ☐

📇 Date:	🕐 Time:	💬 Message:
👤 Caller:		
🏢 Company:		
📞 Phone:		
@ Email:		
🚨 Urgency: ☐ Low ☐ Medium ☐ High		📞 Called ☐

📇 Date:	🕐 Time:	💬 Message:
👤 Caller:		
🏢 Company:		
📞 Phone:		
@ Email:		
🚨 Urgency: ☐ Low ☐ Medium ☐ High		📞 Called ☐

📇 Date:	🕐 Time:	💬 Message:
👤 Caller:		
🏢 Company:		
📞 Phone:		
@ Email:		
🚨 Urgency: ☐ Low ☐ Medium ☐ High		📞 Called ☐

📇 Date:	🕐 Time:	💬 Message:
👤 Caller:		
🏢 Company:		
📞 Phone:		
@ Email:		
🚨 Urgency: ☐ Low ☐ Medium ☐ High		📞 Called ☐

📇 Date:	🕐 Time:	💬 Message:
👤 Caller:		
🏢 Company:		
📞 Phone:		
@ Email:		
🚨 Urgency: ☐ Low ☐ Medium ☐ High		📞 Called ☐

Date:	Time:	Message:
Caller:		
Company:		
Phone:		
Email:		
Urgency: ☐ Low ☐ Medium ☐ High		Called ☐

Date:	Time:	Message:
Caller:		
Company:		
Phone:		
Email:		
Urgency: ☐ Low ☐ Medium ☐ High		Called ☐

Date:	Time:	Message:
Caller:		
Company:		
Phone:		
Email:		
Urgency: ☐ Low ☐ Medium ☐ High		Called ☐

Date:	Time:	Message:
Caller:		
Company:		
Phone:		
Email:		
Urgency: ☐ Low ☐ Medium ☐ High		Called ☐

Date:	Time:	Message:
Caller:		
Company:		
Phone:		
Email:		
Urgency: ☐ Low ☐ Medium ☐ High		Called ☐

📅 Date:	🕐 Time:	💬 Message:
👤 Caller:		
🏢 Company:		
📞 Phone:		
@ Email:		
🔔 Urgency: ☐ Low ☐ Medium ☐ High		📞 Called ☐

📅 Date:	🕐 Time:	💬 Message:
👤 Caller:		
🏢 Company:		
📞 Phone:		
@ Email:		
🔔 Urgency: ☐ Low ☐ Medium ☐ High		📞 Called ☐

📅 Date:	🕐 Time:	💬 Message:
👤 Caller:		
🏢 Company:		
📞 Phone:		
@ Email:		
🔔 Urgency: ☐ Low ☐ Medium ☐ High		📞 Called ☐

📅 Date:	🕐 Time:	💬 Message:
👤 Caller:		
🏢 Company:		
📞 Phone:		
@ Email:		
🔔 Urgency: ☐ Low ☐ Medium ☐ High		📞 Called ☐

📅 Date:	🕐 Time:	💬 Message:
👤 Caller:		
🏢 Company:		
📞 Phone:		
@ Email:		
🔔 Urgency: ☐ Low ☐ Medium ☐ High		📞 Called ☐

📅 Date:	🕐 Time:	💬 Message:
👤 Caller:		
🏢 Company:		
📞 Phone:		
@ Email:		
☼ Urgency: ☐ Low ☐ Medium ☐ High		📞 Called ☐

📅 Date:	🕐 Time:	💬 Message:
👤 Caller:		
🏢 Company:		
📞 Phone:		
@ Email:		
☼ Urgency: ☐ Low ☐ Medium ☐ High		📞 Called ☐

📅 Date:	🕐 Time:	💬 Message:
👤 Caller:		
🏢 Company:		
📞 Phone:		
@ Email:		
☼ Urgency: ☐ Low ☐ Medium ☐ High		📞 Called ☐

📅 Date:	🕐 Time:	💬 Message:
👤 Caller:		
🏢 Company:		
📞 Phone:		
@ Email:		
☼ Urgency: ☐ Low ☐ Medium ☐ High		📞 Called ☐

📅 Date:	🕐 Time:	💬 Message:
👤 Caller:		
🏢 Company:		
📞 Phone:		
@ Email:		
☼ Urgency: ☐ Low ☐ Medium ☐ High		📞 Called ☐

📅 Date:	🕐 Time:	💬 Message:
👤 Caller:		
🏢 Company:		
📞 Phone:		
@ Email:		
🔆 Urgency: ☐ Low ☐ Medium ☐ High		📞 Called ☐

📅 Date:	🕐 Time:	💬 Message:
👤 Caller:		
🏢 Company:		
📞 Phone:		
@ Email:		
🔆 Urgency: ☐ Low ☐ Medium ☐ High		📞 Called ☐

📅 Date:	🕐 Time:	💬 Message:
👤 Caller:		
🏢 Company:		
📞 Phone:		
@ Email:		
🔆 Urgency: ☐ Low ☐ Medium ☐ High		📞 Called ☐

📅 Date:	🕐 Time:	💬 Message:
👤 Caller:		
🏢 Company:		
📞 Phone:		
@ Email:		
🔆 Urgency: ☐ Low ☐ Medium ☐ High		📞 Called ☐

📅 Date:	🕐 Time:	💬 Message:
👤 Caller:		
🏢 Company:		
📞 Phone:		
@ Email:		
🔆 Urgency: ☐ Low ☐ Medium ☐ High		📞 Called ☐

Date: **Time:**

Caller:

Company:

Phone:

Email:

Urgency: ☐ Low   ☐ Medium   ☐ High

Message:

Called ☐

Date: **Time:**

Caller:

Company:

Phone:

Email:

Urgency: ☐ Low   ☐ Medium   ☐ High

Message:

Called ☐

Date: **Time:**

Caller:

Company:

Phone:

Email:

Urgency: ☐ Low   ☐ Medium   ☐ High

Message:

Called ☐

Date: **Time:**

Caller:

Company:

Phone:

Email:

Urgency: ☐ Low   ☐ Medium   ☐ High

Message:

Called ☐

Date: **Time:**

Caller:

Company:

Phone:

Email:

Urgency: ☐ Low   ☐ Medium   ☐ High

Message:

Called ☐

🗓 Date:	⏲ Time:	💬 Message:
👤 Caller:		
🏢 Company:		
📞 Phone:		
@ Email:		
🔆 Urgency: ☐ Low ☐ Medium ☐ High		📞 Called ☐

🗓 Date:	⏲ Time:	💬 Message:
👤 Caller:		
🏢 Company:		
📞 Phone:		
@ Email:		
🔆 Urgency: ☐ Low ☐ Medium ☐ High		📞 Called ☐

🗓 Date:	⏲ Time:	💬 Message:
👤 Caller:		
🏢 Company:		
📞 Phone:		
@ Email:		
🔆 Urgency: ☐ Low ☐ Medium ☐ High		📞 Called ☐

🗓 Date:	⏲ Time:	💬 Message:
👤 Caller:		
🏢 Company:		
📞 Phone:		
@ Email:		
🔆 Urgency: ☐ Low ☐ Medium ☐ High		📞 Called ☐

🗓 Date:	⏲ Time:	💬 Message:
👤 Caller:		
🏢 Company:		
📞 Phone:		
@ Email:		
🔆 Urgency: ☐ Low ☐ Medium ☐ High		📞 Called ☐

Date: **Time:**

Caller:

Company:

Phone:

Email:

Urgency: ☐ Low   ☐ Medium   ☐ High

Message:

Called ☐

Date: **Time:**

Caller:

Company:

Phone:

Email:

Urgency: ☐ Low   ☐ Medium   ☐ High

Message:

Called ☐

Date: **Time:**

Caller:

Company:

Phone:

Email:

Urgency: ☐ Low   ☐ Medium   ☐ High

Message:

Called ☐

Date: **Time:**

Caller:

Company:

Phone:

Email:

Urgency: ☐ Low   ☐ Medium   ☐ High

Message:

Called ☐

Date: **Time:**

Caller:

Company:

Phone:

Email:

Urgency: ☐ Low   ☐ Medium   ☐ High

Message:

Called ☐

📇 Date:	🕐 Time:	💬 Message:
👤 Caller:		
🏢 Company:		
📞 Phone:		
@ Email:		
🔆 Urgency: ☐ Low ☐ Medium ☐ High		📞 Called ☐

📇 Date:	🕐 Time:	💬 Message:
👤 Caller:		
🏢 Company:		
📞 Phone:		
@ Email:		
🔆 Urgency: ☐ Low ☐ Medium ☐ High		📞 Called ☐

📇 Date:	🕐 Time:	💬 Message:
👤 Caller:		
🏢 Company:		
📞 Phone:		
@ Email:		
🔆 Urgency: ☐ Low ☐ Medium ☐ High		📞 Called ☐

📇 Date:	🕐 Time:	💬 Message:
👤 Caller:		
🏢 Company:		
📞 Phone:		
@ Email:		
🔆 Urgency: ☐ Low ☐ Medium ☐ High		📞 Called ☐

📇 Date:	🕐 Time:	💬 Message:
👤 Caller:		
🏢 Company:		
📞 Phone:		
@ Email:		
🔆 Urgency: ☐ Low ☐ Medium ☐ High		📞 Called ☐

Entry 1

Date: _____ **Time:** _____

Caller: _____

Company: _____

Phone: _____

Email: _____

Urgency: ☐ Low ☐ Medium ☐ High

Message:

Called ☐

Entry 2

Date: _____ **Time:** _____

Caller: _____

Company: _____

Phone: _____

Email: _____

Urgency: ☐ Low ☐ Medium ☐ High

Message:

Called ☐

Entry 3

Date: _____ **Time:** _____

Caller: _____

Company: _____

Phone: _____

Email: _____

Urgency: ☐ Low ☐ Medium ☐ High

Message:

Called ☐

Entry 4

Date: _____ **Time:** _____

Caller: _____

Company: _____

Phone: _____

Email: _____

Urgency: ☐ Low ☐ Medium ☐ High

Message:

Called ☐

Entry 5

Date: _____ **Time:** _____

Caller: _____

Company: _____

Phone: _____

Email: _____

Urgency: ☐ Low ☐ Medium ☐ High

Message:

Called ☐

🗓 Date:	🕐 Time:	💬 Message:
👥 Caller:		
🏢 Company:		
📞 Phone:		
@ Email:		
🔔 Urgency: ☐ Low ☐ Medium ☐ High		📞 Called ☐

🗓 Date:	🕐 Time:	💬 Message:
👥 Caller:		
🏢 Company:		
📞 Phone:		
@ Email:		
🔔 Urgency: ☐ Low ☐ Medium ☐ High		📞 Called ☐

🗓 Date:	🕐 Time:	💬 Message:
👥 Caller:		
🏢 Company:		
📞 Phone:		
@ Email:		
🔔 Urgency: ☐ Low ☐ Medium ☐ High		📞 Called ☐

🗓 Date:	🕐 Time:	💬 Message:
👥 Caller:		
🏢 Company:		
📞 Phone:		
@ Email:		
🔔 Urgency: ☐ Low ☐ Medium ☐ High		📞 Called ☐

🗓 Date:	🕐 Time:	💬 Message:
👥 Caller:		
🏢 Company:		
📞 Phone:		
@ Email:		
🔔 Urgency: ☐ Low ☐ Medium ☐ High		📞 Called ☐

Date: **Time:** **Message:**

Caller:

Company:

Phone:

Email:

Urgency: ☐ Low ☐ Medium ☐ High **Called** ☐

Date: **Time:** **Message:**

Caller:

Company:

Phone:

Email:

Urgency: ☐ Low ☐ Medium ☐ High **Called** ☐

Date: **Time:** **Message:**

Caller:

Company:

Phone:

Email:

Urgency: ☐ Low ☐ Medium ☐ High **Called** ☐

Date: **Time:** **Message:**

Caller:

Company:

Phone:

Email:

Urgency: ☐ Low ☐ Medium ☐ High **Called** ☐

Date: **Time:** **Message:**

Caller:

Company:

Phone:

Email:

Urgency: ☐ Low ☐ Medium ☐ High **Called** ☐

📅 Date:	🕐 Time:	💬 Message:
👤 Caller:		
🏢 Company:		
📞 Phone:		
@ Email:		
☀ Urgency: ☐ Low ☐ Medium ☐ High		📞 Called ☐

📅 Date:	🕐 Time:	💬 Message:
👤 Caller:		
🏢 Company:		
📞 Phone:		
@ Email:		
☀ Urgency: ☐ Low ☐ Medium ☐ High		📞 Called ☐

📅 Date:	🕐 Time:	💬 Message:
👤 Caller:		
🏢 Company:		
📞 Phone:		
@ Email:		
☀ Urgency: ☐ Low ☐ Medium ☐ High		📞 Called ☐

📅 Date:	🕐 Time:	💬 Message:
👤 Caller:		
🏢 Company:		
📞 Phone:		
@ Email:		
☀ Urgency: ☐ Low ☐ Medium ☐ High		📞 Called ☐

📅 Date:	🕐 Time:	💬 Message:
👤 Caller:		
🏢 Company:		
📞 Phone:		
@ Email:		
☀ Urgency: ☐ Low ☐ Medium ☐ High		📞 Called ☐

Date: **Time:**   **Message:**

Caller:

Company:

Phone:

Email:

Urgency: ☐ Low   ☐ Medium   ☐ High   **Called** ☐

Date: **Time:**   **Message:**

Caller:

Company:

Phone:

Email:

Urgency: ☐ Low   ☐ Medium   ☐ High   **Called** ☐

Date: **Time:**   **Message:**

Caller:

Company:

Phone:

Email:

Urgency: ☐ Low   ☐ Medium   ☐ High   **Called** ☐

Date: **Time:**   **Message:**

Caller:

Company:

Phone:

Email:

Urgency: ☐ Low   ☐ Medium   ☐ High   **Called** ☐

Date: **Time:**   **Message:**

Caller:

Company:

Phone:

Email:

Urgency: ☐ Low   ☐ Medium   ☐ High   **Called** ☐

📇 Date:	🕐 Time:	💬 Message:
👥 Caller:		
🏢 Company:		
📞 Phone:		
@ Email:		
🔆 Urgency: ☐ Low ☐ Medium ☐ High		📞 Called ☐

📇 Date:	🕐 Time:	💬 Message:
👥 Caller:		
🏢 Company:		
📞 Phone:		
@ Email:		
🔆 Urgency: ☐ Low ☐ Medium ☐ High		📞 Called ☐

📇 Date:	🕐 Time:	💬 Message:
👥 Caller:		
🏢 Company:		
📞 Phone:		
@ Email:		
🔆 Urgency: ☐ Low ☐ Medium ☐ High		📞 Called ☐

📇 Date:	🕐 Time:	💬 Message:
👥 Caller:		
🏢 Company:		
📞 Phone:		
@ Email:		
🔆 Urgency: ☐ Low ☐ Medium ☐ High		📞 Called ☐

📇 Date:	🕐 Time:	💬 Message:
👥 Caller:		
🏢 Company:		
📞 Phone:		
@ Email:		
🔆 Urgency: ☐ Low ☐ Medium ☐ High		📞 Called ☐

Date:	Time:	Message:
Caller:		
Company:		
Phone:		
Email:		
Urgency: ☐ Low ☐ Medium ☐ High		Called ☐

Date:	Time:	Message:
Caller:		
Company:		
Phone:		
Email:		
Urgency: ☐ Low ☐ Medium ☐ High		Called ☐

Date:	Time:	Message:
Caller:		
Company:		
Phone:		
Email:		
Urgency: ☐ Low ☐ Medium ☐ High		Called ☐

Date:	Time:	Message:
Caller:		
Company:		
Phone:		
Email:		
Urgency: ☐ Low ☐ Medium ☐ High		Called ☐

Date:	Time:	Message:
Caller:		
Company:		
Phone:		
Email:		
Urgency: ☐ Low ☐ Medium ☐ High		Called ☐

🗓 Date:	🕐 Time:	💬 Message:
👤 Caller:		
🏢 Company:		
📞 Phone:		
@ Email:		
🚨 Urgency: ☐ Low ☐ Medium ☐ High		📞 Called ☐

🗓 Date:	🕐 Time:	💬 Message:
👤 Caller:		
🏢 Company:		
📞 Phone:		
@ Email:		
🚨 Urgency: ☐ Low ☐ Medium ☐ High		📞 Called ☐

🗓 Date:	🕐 Time:	💬 Message:
👤 Caller:		
🏢 Company:		
📞 Phone:		
@ Email:		
🚨 Urgency: ☐ Low ☐ Medium ☐ High		📞 Called ☐

🗓 Date:	🕐 Time:	💬 Message:
👤 Caller:		
🏢 Company:		
📞 Phone:		
@ Email:		
🚨 Urgency: ☐ Low ☐ Medium ☐ High		📞 Called ☐

🗓 Date:	🕐 Time:	💬 Message:
👤 Caller:		
🏢 Company:		
📞 Phone:		
@ Email:		
🚨 Urgency: ☐ Low ☐ Medium ☐ High		📞 Called ☐

Entry 1

🗓 **Date:**   🕐 **Time:**

👤 **Caller:**

🏢 **Company:**

📞 **Phone:**

@ **Email:**

🔆 **Urgency:**   ☐ Low   ☐ Medium   ☐ High

💬 **Message:**

📞 **Called** ☐

Entry 2

🗓 **Date:**   🕐 **Time:**

👤 **Caller:**

🏢 **Company:**

📞 **Phone:**

@ **Email:**

🔆 **Urgency:**   ☐ Low   ☐ Medium   ☐ High

💬 **Message:**

📞 **Called** ☐

Entry 3

🗓 **Date:**   🕐 **Time:**

👤 **Caller:**

🏢 **Company:**

📞 **Phone:**

@ **Email:**

🔆 **Urgency:**   ☐ Low   ☐ Medium   ☐ High

💬 **Message:**

📞 **Called** ☐

Entry 4

🗓 **Date:**   🕐 **Time:**

👤 **Caller:**

🏢 **Company:**

📞 **Phone:**

@ **Email:**

🔆 **Urgency:**   ☐ Low   ☐ Medium   ☐ High

💬 **Message:**

📞 **Called** ☐

Entry 5

🗓 **Date:**   🕐 **Time:**

👤 **Caller:**

🏢 **Company:**

📞 **Phone:**

@ **Email:**

🔆 **Urgency:**   ☐ Low   ☐ Medium   ☐ High

💬 **Message:**

📞 **Called** ☐

📇 Date:	🕐 Time:	💬 Message:
👥 Caller:		
🏢 Company:		
📞 Phone:		
@ Email:		
☀ Urgency: ☐ Low ☐ Medium ☐ High		📞 Called ☐

📇 Date:	🕐 Time:	💬 Message:
👥 Caller:		
🏢 Company:		
📞 Phone:		
@ Email:		
☀ Urgency: ☐ Low ☐ Medium ☐ High		📞 Called ☐

📇 Date:	🕐 Time:	💬 Message:
👥 Caller:		
🏢 Company:		
📞 Phone:		
@ Email:		
☀ Urgency: ☐ Low ☐ Medium ☐ High		📞 Called ☐

📇 Date:	🕐 Time:	💬 Message:
👥 Caller:		
🏢 Company:		
📞 Phone:		
@ Email:		
☀ Urgency: ☐ Low ☐ Medium ☐ High		📞 Called ☐

📇 Date:	🕐 Time:	💬 Message:
👥 Caller:		
🏢 Company:		
📞 Phone:		
@ Email:		
☀ Urgency: ☐ Low ☐ Medium ☐ High		📞 Called ☐

Date:	Time:	Message:
Caller:		
Company:		
Phone:		
Email:		
Urgency: ☐ Low ☐ Medium ☐ High		Called ☐

Date:	Time:	Message:
Caller:		
Company:		
Phone:		
Email:		
Urgency: ☐ Low ☐ Medium ☐ High		Called ☐

Date:	Time:	Message:
Caller:		
Company:		
Phone:		
Email:		
Urgency: ☐ Low ☐ Medium ☐ High		Called ☐

Date:	Time:	Message:
Caller:		
Company:		
Phone:		
Email:		
Urgency: ☐ Low ☐ Medium ☐ High		Called ☐

Date:	Time:	Message:
Caller:		
Company:		
Phone:		
Email:		
Urgency: ☐ Low ☐ Medium ☐ High		Called ☐

📇 Date:	🕐 Time:	💬 Message:
👤 Caller:		
🏢 Company:		
📞 Phone:		
@ Email:		
🔆 Urgency: ☐ Low ☐ Medium ☐ High		📲 Called ☐

📇 Date:	🕐 Time:	💬 Message:
👤 Caller:		
🏢 Company:		
📞 Phone:		
@ Email:		
🔆 Urgency: ☐ Low ☐ Medium ☐ High		📲 Called ☐

📇 Date:	🕐 Time:	💬 Message:
👤 Caller:		
🏢 Company:		
📞 Phone:		
@ Email:		
🔆 Urgency: ☐ Low ☐ Medium ☐ High		📲 Called ☐

📇 Date:	🕐 Time:	💬 Message:
👤 Caller:		
🏢 Company:		
📞 Phone:		
@ Email:		
🔆 Urgency: ☐ Low ☐ Medium ☐ High		📲 Called ☐

📇 Date:	🕐 Time:	💬 Message:
👤 Caller:		
🏢 Company:		
📞 Phone:		
@ Email:		
🔆 Urgency: ☐ Low ☐ Medium ☐ High		📲 Called ☐

Entry 1

Date: **Time:**

Caller:

Company:

Phone:

Email:

Urgency: ☐ Low   ☐ Medium   ☐ High

Message:

Called ☐

Entry 2

Date: **Time:**

Caller:

Company:

Phone:

Email:

Urgency: ☐ Low   ☐ Medium   ☐ High

Message:

Called ☐

Entry 3

Date: **Time:**

Caller:

Company:

Phone:

Email:

Urgency: ☐ Low   ☐ Medium   ☐ High

Message:

Called ☐

Entry 4

Date: **Time:**

Caller:

Company:

Phone:

Email:

Urgency: ☐ Low   ☐ Medium   ☐ High

Message:

Called ☐

Entry 5

Date: **Time:**

Caller:

Company:

Phone:

Email:

Urgency: ☐ Low   ☐ Medium   ☐ High

Message:

Called ☐

🗓 Date:	🕐 Time:	💬 Message:
👥 Caller:		
🏢 Company:		
📞 Phone:		
@ Email:		
☼ Urgency: ☐ Low ☐ Medium ☐ High		📞 Called ☐

🗓 Date:	🕐 Time:	💬 Message:
👥 Caller:		
🏢 Company:		
📞 Phone:		
@ Email:		
☼ Urgency: ☐ Low ☐ Medium ☐ High		📞 Called ☐

🗓 Date:	🕐 Time:	💬 Message:
👥 Caller:		
🏢 Company:		
📞 Phone:		
@ Email:		
☼ Urgency: ☐ Low ☐ Medium ☐ High		📞 Called ☐

🗓 Date:	🕐 Time:	💬 Message:
👥 Caller:		
🏢 Company:		
📞 Phone:		
@ Email:		
☼ Urgency: ☐ Low ☐ Medium ☐ High		📞 Called ☐

🗓 Date:	🕐 Time:	💬 Message:
👥 Caller:		
🏢 Company:		
📞 Phone:		
@ Email:		
☼ Urgency: ☐ Low ☐ Medium ☐ High		📞 Called ☐

Entry 1

Date: _____ **Time:** _____

Caller: _____

Company: _____

Phone: _____

Email: _____

Urgency: ☐ Low ☐ Medium ☐ High

Message: _____

Called ☐

Entry 2

Date: _____ **Time:** _____

Caller: _____

Company: _____

Phone: _____

Email: _____

Urgency: ☐ Low ☐ Medium ☐ High

Message: _____

Called ☐

Entry 3

Date: _____ **Time:** _____

Caller: _____

Company: _____

Phone: _____

Email: _____

Urgency: ☐ Low ☐ Medium ☐ High

Message: _____

Called ☐

Entry 4

Date: _____ **Time:** _____

Caller: _____

Company: _____

Phone: _____

Email: _____

Urgency: ☐ Low ☐ Medium ☐ High

Message: _____

Called ☐

Entry 5

Date: _____ **Time:** _____

Caller: _____

Company: _____

Phone: _____

Email: _____

Urgency: ☐ Low ☐ Medium ☐ High

Message: _____

Called ☐

📅 Date:	🕐 Time:	💬 Message:
👥 Caller:		
🏢 Company:		
📞 Phone:		
@ Email:		
🔆 Urgency: ☐ Low ☐ Medium ☐ High		📞 Called ☐

📅 Date:	🕐 Time:	💬 Message:
👥 Caller:		
🏢 Company:		
📞 Phone:		
@ Email:		
🔆 Urgency: ☐ Low ☐ Medium ☐ High		📞 Called ☐

📅 Date:	🕐 Time:	💬 Message:
👥 Caller:		
🏢 Company:		
📞 Phone:		
@ Email:		
🔆 Urgency: ☐ Low ☐ Medium ☐ High		📞 Called ☐

📅 Date:	🕐 Time:	💬 Message:
👥 Caller:		
🏢 Company:		
📞 Phone:		
@ Email:		
🔆 Urgency: ☐ Low ☐ Medium ☐ High		📞 Called ☐

📅 Date:	🕐 Time:	💬 Message:
👥 Caller:		
🏢 Company:		
📞 Phone:		
@ Email:		
🔆 Urgency: ☐ Low ☐ Medium ☐ High		📞 Called ☐

Date:	⏱ Time:	💬 Message:
👤 Caller:		
🏢 Company:		
📞 Phone:		
@ Email:		
🚨 Urgency: ☐ Low ☐ Medium ☐ High		📞 Called ☐

Date:	⏱ Time:	💬 Message:
Caller:		
🏢 Company:		
📞 Phone:		
@ Email:		
🚨 Urgency: ☐ Low ☐ Medium ☐ High		📞 Called ☐

Date:	⏱ Time:	💬 Message:
👤 Caller:		
🏢 Company:		
📞 Phone:		
@ Email:		
🚨 Urgency: ☐ Low ☐ Medium ☐ High		📞 Called ☐

Date:	⏱ Time:	💬 Message:
👤 Caller:		
🏢 Company:		
📞 Phone:		
@ Email:		
🚨 Urgency: ☐ Low ☐ Medium ☐ High		📞 Called ☐

Date:	⏱ Time:	💬 Message:
👤 Caller:		
🏢 Company:		
📞 Phone:		
@ Email:		
🚨 Urgency: ☐ Low ☐ Medium ☐ High		📞 Called ☐

📅 Date:	🕐 Time:	💬 Message:
👤 Caller:		
🏢 Company:		
📞 Phone:		
@ Email:		
🔆 Urgency: ☐ Low ☐ Medium ☐ High		📞 Called ☐

📅 Date:	🕐 Time:	💬 Message:
👤 Caller:		
🏢 Company:		
📞 Phone:		
@ Email:		
🔆 Urgency: ☐ Low ☐ Medium ☐ High		📞 Called ☐

📅 Date:	🕐 Time:	💬 Message:
👤 Caller:		
🏢 Company:		
📞 Phone:		
@ Email:		
🔆 Urgency: ☐ Low ☐ Medium ☐ High		📞 Called ☐

📅 Date:	🕐 Time:	💬 Message:
👤 Caller:		
🏢 Company:		
📞 Phone:		
@ Email:		
🔆 Urgency: ☐ Low ☐ Medium ☐ High		📞 Called ☐

📅 Date:	🕐 Time:	💬 Message:
👤 Caller:		
🏢 Company:		
📞 Phone:		
@ Email:		
🔆 Urgency: ☐ Low ☐ Medium ☐ High		📞 Called ☐

🕮 Date:	🕐 Time:	💬 Message:
Caller:		
🏢 Company:		
📞 Phone:		
📧 Email:		
☼ Urgency: ☐ Low ☐ Medium ☐ High		📞 Called ☐

🕮 Date:	🕐 Time:	💬 Message:
👤 Caller:		
🏢 Company:		
📞 Phone:		
@ Email:		
☼ Urgency: ☐ Low ☐ Medium ☐ High		📞 Called ☐

🕮 Date:	🕐 Time:	💬 Message:
👤 Caller:		
🏢 Company:		
📞 Phone:		
@ Email:		
☼ Urgency: ☐ Low ☐ Medium ☐ High		📞 Called ☐

🕮 Date:	🕐 Time:	💬 Message:
👤 Caller:		
🏢 Company:		
📞 Phone:		
@ Email:		
☼ Urgency: ☐ Low ☐ Medium ☐ High		📞 Called ☐

🕮 Date:	🕐 Time:	💬 Message:
👤 Caller:		
🏢 Company:		
📞 Phone:		
@ Email:		
☼ Urgency: ☐ Low ☐ Medium ☐ High		📞 Called ☐

🖩 Date:	🕐 Time:	💬 Message:
👤 Caller:		
🏢 Company:		
📞 Phone:		
@ Email:		
🔆 Urgency: ☐ Low ☐ Medium ☐ High		📞 Called ☐

🖩 Date:	🕐 Time:	💬 Message:
👤 Caller:		
🏢 Company:		
📞 Phone:		
@ Email:		
🔆 Urgency: ☐ Low ☐ Medium ☐ High		📞 Called ☐

🖩 Date:	🕐 Time:	💬 Message:
👤 Caller:		
🏢 Company:		
📞 Phone:		
@ Email:		
🔆 Urgency: ☐ Low ☐ Medium ☐ High		📞 Called ☐

🖩 Date:	🕐 Time:	💬 Message:
👤 Caller:		
🏢 Company:		
📞 Phone:		
@ Email:		
🔆 Urgency: ☐ Low ☐ Medium ☐ High		📞 Called ☐

🖩 Date:	🕐 Time:	💬 Message:
👤 Caller:		
🏢 Company:		
📞 Phone:		
@ Email:		
🔆 Urgency: ☐ Low ☐ Medium ☐ High		📞 Called ☐

Date: **Time:**

Caller:

Company:

Phone:

Email:

Urgency: ☐ Low   ☐ Medium   ☐ High

Message:

Called ☐

Date: **Time:**

Caller:

Company:

Phone:

Email:

Urgency: ☐ Low   ☐ Medium   ☐ High

Message:

Called ☐

Date: **Time:**

Caller:

Company:

Phone:

Email:

Urgency: ☐ Low   ☐ Medium   ☐ High

Message:

Called ☐

Date: **Time:**

Caller:

Company:

Phone:

Email:

Urgency: ☐ Low   ☐ Medium   ☐ High

Message:

Called ☐

Date: **Time:**

Caller:

Company:

Phone:

Email:

Urgency: ☐ Low   ☐ Medium   ☐ High

Message:

Called ☐

🗓 Date:	🕐 Time:	💬 Message:
👤 Caller:		
🏢 Company:		
📞 Phone:		
@ Email:		
☀ Urgency: ☐ Low ☐ Medium ☐ High		📞 Called ☐

🗓 Date:	🕐 Time:	💬 Message:
👤 Caller:		
🏢 Company:		
📞 Phone:		
@ Email:		
☀ Urgency: ☐ Low ☐ Medium ☐ High		📞 Called ☐

🗓 Date:	🕐 Time:	💬 Message:
👤 Caller:		
🏢 Company:		
📞 Phone:		
@ Email:		
☀ Urgency: ☐ Low ☐ Medium ☐ High		📞 Called ☐

🗓 Date:	🕐 Time:	💬 Message:
👤 Caller:		
🏢 Company:		
📞 Phone:		
@ Email:		
☀ Urgency: ☐ Low ☐ Medium ☐ High		📞 Called ☐

🗓 Date:	🕐 Time:	💬 Message:
👤 Caller:		
🏢 Company:		
📞 Phone:		
@ Email:		
☀ Urgency: ☐ Low ☐ Medium ☐ High		📞 Called ☐

📅 Date: 🕐 Time:	💬 Message:
👤 Caller:	
🏢 Company:	
📞 Phone:	
@ Email:	
🚨 Urgency: ☐ Low ☐ Medium ☐ High	📞 Called ☐

📅 Date: 🕐 Time:	💬 Message:
👤 Caller:	
🏢 Company:	
📞 Phone:	
@ Email:	
🚨 Urgency: ☐ Low ☐ Medium ☐ High	📞 Called ☐

📅 Date: 🕐 Time:	💬 Message:
👤 Caller:	
🏢 Company:	
📞 Phone:	
@ Email:	
🚨 Urgency: ☐ Low ☐ Medium ☐ High	📞 Called ☐

📅 Date: 🕐 Time:	💬 Message:
👤 Caller:	
🏢 Company:	
📞 Phone:	
@ Email:	
🚨 Urgency: ☐ Low ☐ Medium ☐ High	📞 Called ☐

📅 Date: 🕐 Time:	💬 Message:
👤 Caller:	
🏢 Company:	
📞 Phone:	
@ Email:	
🚨 Urgency: ☐ Low ☐ Medium ☐ High	📞 Called ☐

📠 Date:	🕐 Time:	💬 Message:
👥 Caller:		
🏢 Company:		
📞 Phone:		
@ Email:		
🔆 Urgency: ☐ Low ☐ Medium ☐ High		📞 Called ☐

📠 Date:	🕐 Time:	💬 Message:
👥 Caller:		
🏢 Company:		
📞 Phone:		
@ Email:		
🔆 Urgency: ☐ Low ☐ Medium ☐ High		📞 Called ☐

📠 Date:	🕐 Time:	💬 Message:
👥 Caller:		
🏢 Company:		
📞 Phone:		
@ Email:		
🔆 Urgency: ☐ Low ☐ Medium ☐ High		📞 Called ☐

📠 Date:	🕐 Time:	💬 Message:
👥 Caller:		
🏢 Company:		
📞 Phone:		
@ Email:		
🔆 Urgency: ☐ Low ☐ Medium ☐ High		📞 Called ☐

📠 Date:	🕐 Time:	💬 Message:
👥 Caller:		
🏢 Company:		
📞 Phone:		
@ Email:		
🔆 Urgency: ☐ Low ☐ Medium ☐ High		📞 Called ☐

📅 Date:	🕐 Time:	💬 Message:
📞 Caller:		
🏢 Company:		
📞 Phone:		
✉ Email:		
⚡ Urgency: ☐ Low ☐ Medium ☐ High		📞 Called ☐

📅 Date:	🕐 Time:	💬 Message:
📞 Caller:		
🏢 Company:		
📞 Phone:		
✉ Email:		
⚡ Urgency: ☐ Low ☐ Medium ☐ High		📞 Called ☐

📅 Date:	🕐 Time:	💬 Message:
📞 Caller:		
🏢 Company:		
📞 Phone:		
@ Email:		
⚡ Urgency: ☐ Low ☐ Medium ☐ High		📞 Called ☐

📅 Date:	🕐 Time:	💬 Message:
📞 Caller:		
🏢 Company:		
📞 Phone:		
@ Email:		
⚡ Urgency: ☐ Low ☐ Medium ☐ High		📞 Called ☐

📅 Date:	🕐 Time:	💬 Message:
📞 Caller:		
🏢 Company:		
📞 Phone:		
@ Email:		
⚡ Urgency: ☐ Low ☐ Medium ☐ High		📞 Called ☐

📇 Date:	🕐 Time:
👥 Caller:	
🏛 Company:	
📞 Phone:	
@ Email:	
🔆 Urgency: ☐ Low ☐ Medium ☐ High	

💬 Message:

📞 Called ☐

📇 Date:	🕐 Time:
👥 Caller:	
🏛 Company:	
📞 Phone:	
@ Email:	
🔆 Urgency: ☐ Low ☐ Medium ☐ High	

💬 Message:

📞 Called ☐

📇 Date:	🕐 Time:
👥 Caller:	
🏛 Company:	
📞 Phone:	
@ Email:	
🔆 Urgency: ☐ Low ☐ Medium ☐ High	

💬 Message:

📞 Called ☐

📇 Date:	🕐 Time:
👥 Caller:	
🏛 Company:	
📞 Phone:	
@ Email:	
🔆 Urgency: ☐ Low ☐ Medium ☐ High	

💬 Message:

📞 Called ☐

📇 Date:	🕐 Time:
👥 Caller:	
🏛 Company:	
📞 Phone:	
@ Email:	
🔆 Urgency: ☐ Low ☐ Medium ☐ High	

💬 Message:

📞 Called ☐

Date: **Time:** **Message:**

Caller:

Company:

Phone:

Email:

Urgency: ☐ Low ☐ Medium ☐ High **Called** ☐

Date: **Time:** **Message:**

Caller:

Company:

Phone:

Email:

Urgency: ☐ Low ☐ Medium ☐ High **Called** ☐

Date: **Time:** **Message:**

Caller:

Company:

Phone:

Email:

Urgency: ☐ Low ☐ Medium ☐ High **Called** ☐

Date: **Time:** **Message:**

Caller:

Company:

Phone:

Email:

Urgency: ☐ Low ☐ Medium ☐ High **Called** ☐

Date: **Time:** **Message:**

Caller:

Company:

Phone:

Email:

Urgency: ☐ Low ☐ Medium ☐ High **Called** ☐

📅 Date:	🕐 Time:	💬 Message:
👥 Caller:		
🏢 Company:		
📞 Phone:		
@ Email:		
🔆 Urgency: ☐ Low ☐ Medium ☐ High		📲 Called ☐

📅 Date:	🕐 Time:	💬 Message:
👥 Caller:		
🏢 Company:		
📞 Phone:		
@ Email:		
🔆 Urgency: ☐ Low ☐ Medium ☐ High		📲 Called ☐

📅 Date:	🕐 Time:	💬 Message:
👥 Caller:		
🏢 Company:		
📞 Phone:		
@ Email:		
🔆 Urgency: ☐ Low ☐ Medium ☐ High		📲 Called ☐

📅 Date:	🕐 Time:	💬 Message:
👥 Caller:		
🏢 Company:		
📞 Phone:		
@ Email:		
🔆 Urgency: ☐ Low ☐ Medium ☐ High		📲 Called ☐

📅 Date:	🕐 Time:	💬 Message:
👥 Caller:		
🏢 Company:		
📞 Phone:		
@ Email:		
🔆 Urgency: ☐ Low ☐ Medium ☐ High		📲 Called ☐

📅 Date:	🕐 Time:	💬 Message:
📞 Caller:		
🏢 Company:		
📞 Phone:		
@ Email:		
🔔 Urgency: ☐ Low ☐ Medium ☐ High		📞 Called ☐

📅 Date:	🕐 Time:	💬 Message:
📞 Caller:		
🏢 Company:		
📞 Phone:		
@ Email:		
🔔 Urgency: ☐ Low ☐ Medium ☐ High		📞 Called ☐

📅 Date:	🕐 Time:	💬 Message:
📞 Caller:		
🏢 Company:		
📞 Phone:		
@ Email:		
🔔 Urgency: ☐ Low ☐ Medium ☐ High		📞 Called ☐

📅 Date:	🕐 Time:	💬 Message:
📞 Caller:		
🏢 Company:		
📞 Phone:		
@ Email:		
🔔 Urgency: ☐ Low ☐ Medium ☐ High		📞 Called ☐

📅 Date:	🕐 Time:	💬 Message:
📞 Caller:		
🏢 Company:		
📞 Phone:		
@ Email:		
🔔 Urgency: ☐ Low ☐ Medium ☐ High		📞 Called ☐

📅 Date:	🕐 Time:	💬 Message:
👥 Caller:		
🏢 Company:		
📞 Phone:		
@ Email:		
🔆 Urgency: ☐ Low ☐ Medium ☐ High		📞 Called ☐

📅 Date:	🕐 Time:	💬 Message:
👥 Caller:		
🏢 Company:		
📞 Phone:		
@ Email:		
🔆 Urgency: ☐ Low ☐ Medium ☐ High		📞 Called ☐

📅 Date:	🕐 Time:	💬 Message:
👥 Caller:		
🏢 Company:		
📞 Phone:		
@ Email:		
🔆 Urgency: ☐ Low ☐ Medium ☐ High		📞 Called ☐

📅 Date:	🕐 Time:	💬 Message:
👥 Caller:		
🏢 Company:		
📞 Phone:		
@ Email:		
🔆 Urgency: ☐ Low ☐ Medium ☐ High		📞 Called ☐

📅 Date:	🕐 Time:	💬 Message:
👥 Caller:		
🏢 Company:		
📞 Phone:		
@ Email:		
🔆 Urgency: ☐ Low ☐ Medium ☐ High		📞 Called ☐

Date: **Time:**

Caller:

Company:

Phone:

Email:

Urgency: ☐ Low   ☐ Medium   ☐ High

Message:

Called ☐

Date: **Time:**

Caller:

Company:

Phone:

Email:

Urgency: ☐ Low   ☐ Medium   ☐ High

Message:

Called ☐

Date: **Time:**

Caller:

Company:

Phone:

Email:

Urgency: ☐ Low   ☐ Medium   ☐ High

Message:

Called ☐

Date: **Time:**

Caller:

Company:

Phone:

Email:

Urgency: ☐ Low   ☐ Medium   ☐ High

Message:

Called ☐

Date: **Time:**

Caller:

Company:

Phone:

Email:

Urgency: ☐ Low   ☐ Medium   ☐ High

Message:

Called ☐

🗓 Date:	⏰ Time:	💬 Message:
👤 Caller:		
🏢 Company:		
📞 Phone:		
@ Email:		
🔔 Urgency: ☐ Low ☐ Medium ☐ High		📞 Called ☐

🗓 Date:	⏰ Time:	💬 Message:
👤 Caller:		
🏢 Company:		
📞 Phone:		
@ Email:		
🔔 Urgency: ☐ Low ☐ Medium ☐ High		📞 Called ☐

🗓 Date:	⏰ Time:	💬 Message:
👤 Caller:		
🏢 Company:		
📞 Phone:		
@ Email:		
🔔 Urgency: ☐ Low ☐ Medium ☐ High		📞 Called ☐

🗓 Date:	⏰ Time:	💬 Message:
👤 Caller:		
🏢 Company:		
📞 Phone:		
@ Email:		
🔔 Urgency: ☐ Low ☐ Medium ☐ High		📞 Called ☐

🗓 Date:	⏰ Time:	💬 Message:
👤 Caller:		
🏢 Company:		
📞 Phone:		
@ Email:		
🔔 Urgency: ☐ Low ☐ Medium ☐ High		📞 Called ☐

Entry 1

📅 **Date:** _____ 🕐 **Time:** _____

👤 **Caller:** _____

🏢 **Company:** _____

📞 **Phone:** _____

@ **Email:** _____

🔆 **Urgency:** ☐ Low ☐ Medium ☐ High

💬 **Message:**

📞 Called ☐

Entry 2

📅 **Date:** _____ 🕐 **Time:** _____

👤 **Caller:** _____

🏢 **Company:** _____

📞 **Phone:** _____

@ **Email:** _____

🔆 **Urgency:** ☐ Low ☐ Medium ☐ High

💬 **Message:**

📞 Called ☐

Entry 3

📅 **Date:** _____ 🕐 **Time:** _____

👤 **Caller:** _____

🏢 **Company:** _____

📞 **Phone:** _____

@ **Email:** _____

🔆 **Urgency:** ☐ Low ☐ Medium ☐ High

💬 **Message:**

📞 Called ☐

Entry 4

📅 **Date:** _____ 🕐 **Time:** _____

👤 **Caller:** _____

🏢 **Company:** _____

📞 **Phone:** _____

@ **Email:** _____

🔆 **Urgency:** ☐ Low ☐ Medium ☐ High

💬 **Message:**

📞 Called ☐

Entry 5

📅 **Date:** _____ 🕐 **Time:** _____

👤 **Caller:** _____

🏢 **Company:** _____

📞 **Phone:** _____

@ **Email:** _____

🔆 **Urgency:** ☐ Low ☐ Medium ☐ High

💬 **Message:**

📞 Called ☐

📅 Date:	🕐 Time:	💬 Message:
👥 Caller:		
🏢 Company:		
🕐 Phone:		
@ Email:		
🔆 Urgency: ☐ Low ☐ Medium ☐ High		📞 Called ☐

📅 Date:	🕐 Time:	💬 Message:
👥 Caller:		
🏢 Company:		
🕐 Phone:		
@ Email:		
🔆 Urgency: ☐ Low ☐ Medium ☐ High		📞 Called ☐

📅 Date:	🕐 Time:	💬 Message:
👥 Caller:		
🏢 Company:		
🕐 Phone:		
@ Email:		
🔆 Urgency: ☐ Low ☐ Medium ☐ High		📞 Called ☐

📅 Date:	🕐 Time:	💬 Message:
👥 Caller:		
🏢 Company:		
🕐 Phone:		
@ Email:		
🔆 Urgency: ☐ Low ☐ Medium ☐ High		📞 Called ☐

📅 Date:	🕐 Time:	💬 Message:
👥 Caller:		
🏢 Company:		
🕐 Phone:		
@ Email:		
🔆 Urgency: ☐ Low ☐ Medium ☐ High		📞 Called ☐

Message Log Entry 1

🗓 Date: _____ 🕐 Time: _____

👤 Caller: _____

🏛 Company: _____

📞 Phone: _____

@ Email: _____

🚨 Urgency: ☐ Low ☐ Medium ☐ High

💬 Message: _____

📞 Called ☐

Message Log Entry 2

🗓 Date: _____ 🕐 Time: _____

👤 Caller: _____

🏛 Company: _____

📞 Phone: _____

@ Email: _____

🚨 Urgency: ☐ Low ☐ Medium ☐ High

💬 Message: _____

📞 Called ☐

Message Log Entry 3

🗓 Date: _____ 🕐 Time: _____

👤 Caller: _____

🏛 Company: _____

📞 Phone: _____

@ Email: _____

🚨 Urgency: ☐ Low ☐ Medium ☐ High

💬 Message: _____

📞 Called ☐

Message Log Entry 4

🗓 Date: _____ 🕐 Time: _____

👤 Caller: _____

🏛 Company: _____

📞 Phone: _____

@ Email: _____

🚨 Urgency: ☐ Low ☐ Medium ☐ High

💬 Message: _____

📞 Called ☐

Message Log Entry 5

🗓 Date: _____ 🕐 Time: _____

👤 Caller: _____

🏛 Company: _____

📞 Phone: _____

@ Email: _____

🚨 Urgency: ☐ Low ☐ Medium ☐ High

💬 Message: _____

📞 Called ☐

🗓 Date:	🕐 Time:	💬 Message:
👥 Caller:		
🏢 Company:		
📞 Phone:		
@ Email:		
🔆 Urgency: ☐ Low ☐ Medium ☐ High		📞 Called ☐

🗓 Date:	🕐 Time:	💬 Message:
👥 Caller:		
🏢 Company:		
📞 Phone:		
@ Email:		
🔆 Urgency: ☐ Low ☐ Medium ☐ High		📞 Called ☐

🗓 Date:	🕐 Time:	💬 Message:
👥 Caller:		
🏢 Company:		
📞 Phone:		
@ Email:		
🔆 Urgency: ☐ Low ☐ Medium ☐ High		📞 Called ☐

🗓 Date:	🕐 Time:	💬 Message:
👥 Caller:		
🏢 Company:		
📞 Phone:		
@ Email:		
🔆 Urgency: ☐ Low ☐ Medium ☐ High		📞 Called ☐

🗓 Date:	🕐 Time:	💬 Message:
👥 Caller:		
🏢 Company:		
📞 Phone:		
@ Email:		
🔆 Urgency: ☐ Low ☐ Medium ☐ High		📞 Called ☐

Date: **Time:**

Caller:

Company:

Phone:

@ Email:

Urgency: ☐ Low ☐ Medium ☐ High

Message:

Called ☐

Date: **Time:**

Caller:

Company:

Phone:

@ Email:

Urgency: ☐ Low ☐ Medium ☐ High

Message:

Called ☐

Date: **Time:**

Caller:

Company:

Phone:

@ Email:

Urgency: ☐ Low ☐ Medium ☐ High

Message:

Called ☐

Date: **Time:**

Caller:

Company:

Phone:

@ Email:

Urgency: ☐ Low ☐ Medium ☐ High

Message:

Called ☐

Date: **Time:**

Caller:

Company:

Phone:

@ Email:

Urgency: ☐ Low ☐ Medium ☐ High

Message:

Called ☐

📅 Date:	🕐 Time:	💬 Message:
👥 Caller:		
🏢 Company:		
📞 Phone:		
@ Email:		
🔅 Urgency: ☐ Low ☐ Medium ☐ High		📞 Called ☐

📅 Date:	🕐 Time:	💬 Message:
👥 Caller:		
🏢 Company:		
📞 Phone:		
@ Email:		
🔅 Urgency: ☐ Low ☐ Medium ☐ High		📞 Called ☐

📅 Date:	🕐 Time:	💬 Message:
👥 Caller:		
🏢 Company:		
📞 Phone:		
@ Email:		
🔅 Urgency: ☐ Low ☐ Medium ☐ High		📞 Called ☐

📅 Date:	🕐 Time:	💬 Message:
👥 Caller:		
🏢 Company:		
📞 Phone:		
@ Email:		
🔅 Urgency: ☐ Low ☐ Medium ☐ High		📞 Called ☐

📅 Date:	🕐 Time:	💬 Message:
👥 Caller:		
🏢 Company:		
📞 Phone:		
@ Email:		
🔅 Urgency: ☐ Low ☐ Medium ☐ High		📞 Called ☐

Date: Time:	Message:
Caller:	
Company:	
Phone:	
Email:	
Urgency: ☐ Low ☐ Medium ☐ High	Called ☐

Date: Time:	Message:
Caller:	
Company:	
Phone:	
Email:	
Urgency: ☐ Low ☐ Medium ☐ High	Called ☐

Date: Time:	Message:
Caller:	
Company:	
Phone:	
Email:	
Urgency: ☐ Low ☐ Medium ☐ High	Called ☐

Date: Time:	Message:
Caller:	
Company:	
Phone:	
Email:	
Urgency: ☐ Low ☐ Medium ☐ High	Called ☐

Date: Time:	Message:
Caller:	
Company:	
Phone:	
Email:	
Urgency: ☐ Low ☐ Medium ☐ High	Called ☐

📅 Date:	🕐 Time:	💬 Message:
👥 Caller:		
🏢 Company:		
📞 Phone:		
@ Email:		
🔆 Urgency: ☐ Low ☐ Medium ☐ High		📞 Called ☐

📅 Date:	🕐 Time:	💬 Message:
👥 Caller:		
🏢 Company:		
📞 Phone:		
@ Email:		
🔆 Urgency: ☐ Low ☐ Medium ☐ High		📞 Called ☐

📅 Date:	🕐 Time:	💬 Message:
👥 Caller:		
🏢 Company:		
📞 Phone:		
@ Email:		
🔆 Urgency: ☐ Low ☐ Medium ☐ High		📞 Called ☐

📅 Date:	🕐 Time:	💬 Message:
👥 Caller:		
🏢 Company:		
📞 Phone:		
@ Email:		
🔆 Urgency: ☐ Low ☐ Medium ☐ High		📞 Called ☐

📅 Date:	🕐 Time:	💬 Message:
👥 Caller:		
🏢 Company:		
📞 Phone:		
@ Email:		
🔆 Urgency: ☐ Low ☐ Medium ☐ High		📞 Called ☐

Date: **Time:** **Message:**

Caller:

Company:

Phone:

Email:

Urgency: ☐ Low ☐ Medium ☐ High **Called** ☐

Date: **Time:** **Message:**

Caller:

Company:

Phone:

Email:

Urgency: ☐ Low ☐ Medium ☐ High **Called** ☐

Date: **Time:** **Message:**

Caller:

Company:

Phone:

Email:

Urgency: ☐ Low ☐ Medium ☐ High **Called** ☐

Date: **Time:** **Message:**

Caller:

Company:

Phone:

Email:

Urgency: ☐ Low ☐ Medium ☐ High **Called** ☐

Date: **Time:** **Message:**

Caller:

Company:

Phone:

Email:

Urgency: ☐ Low ☐ Medium ☐ High **Called** ☐

🗓 Date: 🕐 Time:	💬 Message:
👥 Caller:	
🏢 Company:	
📞 Phone:	
@ Email:	
🔆 Urgency: ☐ Low ☐ Medium ☐ High	📲 Called ☐

🗓 Date: 🕐 Time:	💬 Message:
👥 Caller:	
🏢 Company:	
📞 Phone:	
@ Email:	
🔆 Urgency: ☐ Low ☐ Medium ☐ High	📲 Called ☐

🗓 Date: 🕐 Time:	💬 Message:
👥 Caller:	
🏢 Company:	
📞 Phone:	
@ Email:	
🔆 Urgency: ☐ Low ☐ Medium ☐ High	📲 Called ☐

🗓 Date: 🕐 Time:	💬 Message:
👥 Caller:	
🏢 Company:	
📞 Phone:	
@ Email:	
🔆 Urgency: ☐ Low ☐ Medium ☐ High	📲 Called ☐

🗓 Date: 🕐 Time:	💬 Message:
👥 Caller:	
🏢 Company:	
📞 Phone:	
@ Email:	
🔆 Urgency: ☐ Low ☐ Medium ☐ High	📲 Called ☐

Entry 1

🗓 Date: _____ 🕐 Time: _____

👤 Caller: _____

🏢 Company: _____

📞 Phone: _____

@ Email: _____

🔔 Urgency: ☐ Low ☐ Medium ☐ High

💬 Message: _____

📞 Called ☐

Entry 2

🗓 Date: _____ 🕐 Time: _____

👤 Caller: _____

🏢 Company: _____

📞 Phone: _____

@ Email: _____

🔔 Urgency: ☐ Low ☐ Medium ☐ High

💬 Message: _____

📞 Called ☐

Entry 3

🗓 Date: _____ 🕐 Time: _____

👤 Caller: _____

🏢 Company: _____

📞 Phone: _____

@ Email: _____

🔔 Urgency: ☐ Low ☐ Medium ☐ High

💬 Message: _____

📞 Called ☐

Entry 4

🗓 Date: _____ 🕐 Time: _____

👤 Caller: _____

🏢 Company: _____

📞 Phone: _____

@ Email: _____

🔔 Urgency: ☐ Low ☐ Medium ☐ High

💬 Message: _____

📞 Called ☐

Entry 5

🗓 Date: _____ 🕐 Time: _____

👤 Caller: _____

🏢 Company: _____

📞 Phone: _____

@ Email: _____

🔔 Urgency: ☐ Low ☐ Medium ☐ High

💬 Message: _____

📞 Called ☐

📅 Date: ⏰ Time:	💬 Message:
👥 Caller:	
🏢 Company:	
📞 Phone:	
@ Email:	
🔆 Urgency: ☐ Low ☐ Medium ☐ High	📞 Called ☐

📅 Date: ⏰ Time:	💬 Message:
👥 Caller:	
🏢 Company:	
📞 Phone:	
@ Email:	
🔆 Urgency: ☐ Low ☐ Medium ☐ High	📞 Called ☐

📅 Date: ⏰ Time:	💬 Message:
👥 Caller:	
🏢 Company:	
📞 Phone:	
@ Email:	
🔆 Urgency: ☐ Low ☐ Medium ☐ High	📞 Called ☐

📅 Date: ⏰ Time:	💬 Message:
👥 Caller:	
🏢 Company:	
📞 Phone:	
@ Email:	
🔆 Urgency: ☐ Low ☐ Medium ☐ High	📞 Called ☐

📅 Date: ⏰ Time:	💬 Message:
👥 Caller:	
🏢 Company:	
📞 Phone:	
@ Email:	
🔆 Urgency: ☐ Low ☐ Medium ☐ High	📞 Called ☐

🗓 Date: ⏱ Time:	💬 Message:
👤 Caller:	
🏢 Company:	
📞 Phone:	
@ Email:	
☼ Urgency: ☐ Low ☐ Medium ☐ High	📞 Called ☐

🗓 Date: ⏱ Time:	💬 Message:
👤 Caller:	
🏢 Company:	
📞 Phone:	
@ Email:	
☼ Urgency: ☐ Low ☐ Medium ☐ High	📞 Called ☐

🗓 Date: ⏱ Time:	💬 Message:
👤 Caller:	
🏢 Company:	
📞 Phone:	
@ Email:	
☼ Urgency: ☐ Low ☐ Medium ☐ High	📞 Called ☐

🗓 Date: ⏱ Time:	💬 Message:
👤 Caller:	
🏢 Company:	
📞 Phone:	
@ Email:	
☼ Urgency: ☐ Low ☐ Medium ☐ High	📞 Called ☐

🗓 Date: ⏱ Time:	💬 Message:
👤 Caller:	
🏢 Company:	
📞 Phone:	
@ Email:	
☼ Urgency: ☐ Low ☐ Medium ☐ High	📞 Called ☐

📅 Date:	🕐 Time:	💬 Message:
👥 Caller:		
🏢 Company:		
📞 Phone:		
@ Email:		
🔆 Urgency: ☐ Low ☐ Medium ☐ High		📞 Called ☐

📅 Date:	🕐 Time:	💬 Message:
👥 Caller:		
🏢 Company:		
📞 Phone:		
@ Email:		
🔆 Urgency: ☐ Low ☐ Medium ☐ High		📞 Called ☐

📅 Date:	🕐 Time:	💬 Message:
👥 Caller:		
🏢 Company:		
📞 Phone:		
@ Email:		
🔆 Urgency: ☐ Low ☐ Medium ☐ High		📞 Called ☐

📅 Date:	🕐 Time:	💬 Message:
👥 Caller:		
🏢 Company:		
📞 Phone:		
@ Email:		
🔆 Urgency: ☐ Low ☐ Medium ☐ High		📞 Called ☐

📅 Date:	🕐 Time:	💬 Message:
👥 Caller:		
🏢 Company:		
📞 Phone:		
@ Email:		
🔆 Urgency: ☐ Low ☐ Medium ☐ High		📞 Called ☐

Date:	Time:	Message:
Caller:		
Company:		
Phone:		
Email:		
Urgency: ☐ Low ☐ Medium ☐ High		Called ☐

Date:	Time:	Message:
Caller:		
Company:		
Phone:		
Email:		
Urgency: ☐ Low ☐ Medium ☐ High		Called ☐

Date:	Time:	Message:
Caller:		
Company:		
Phone:		
Email:		
Urgency: ☐ Low ☐ Medium ☐ High		Called ☐

Date:	Time:	Message:
Caller:		
Company:		
Phone:		
Email:		
Urgency: ☐ Low ☐ Medium ☐ High		Called ☐

Date:	Time:	Message:
Caller:		
Company:		
Phone:		
Email:		
Urgency: ☐ Low ☐ Medium ☐ High		Called ☐

📅 Date:	🕐 Time:	💬 Message:
👥 Caller:		
🏢 Company:		
📞 Phone:		
@ Email:		
🔆 Urgency: ☐ Low ☐ Medium ☐ High		📞 Called ☐

📅 Date:	🕐 Time:	💬 Message:
👥 Caller:		
🏢 Company:		
📞 Phone:		
@ Email:		
🔆 Urgency: ☐ Low ☐ Medium ☐ High		📞 Called ☐

📅 Date:	🕐 Time:	💬 Message:
👥 Caller:		
🏢 Company:		
📞 Phone:		
@ Email:		
🔆 Urgency: ☐ Low ☐ Medium ☐ High		📞 Called ☐

📅 Date:	🕐 Time:	💬 Message:
👥 Caller:		
🏢 Company:		
📞 Phone:		
@ Email:		
🔆 Urgency: ☐ Low ☐ Medium ☐ High		📞 Called ☐

📅 Date:	🕐 Time:	💬 Message:
👥 Caller:		
🏢 Company:		
📞 Phone:		
@ Email:		
🔆 Urgency: ☐ Low ☐ Medium ☐ High		📞 Called ☐

📅 Date:	🕐 Time:	💬 Message:
👤 Caller:		
🏢 Company:		
📞 Phone:		
✉ Email:		
🔔 Urgency: ☐ Low ☐ Medium ☐ High		📞 Called ☐

📅 Date:	🕐 Time:	💬 Message:
👤 Caller:		
🏢 Company:		
📞 Phone:		
✉ Email:		
🔔 Urgency: ☐ Low ☐ Medium ☐ High		📞 Called ☐

📅 Date:	🕐 Time:	💬 Message:
👤 Caller:		
🏢 Company:		
📞 Phone:		
✉ Email:		
🔔 Urgency: ☐ Low ☐ Medium ☐ High		📞 Called ☐

📅 Date:	🕐 Time:	💬 Message:
👤 Caller:		
🏢 Company:		
📞 Phone:		
✉ Email:		
🔔 Urgency: ☐ Low ☐ Medium ☐ High		📞 Called ☐

📅 Date:	🕐 Time:	💬 Message:
👤 Caller:		
🏢 Company:		
📞 Phone:		
✉ Email:		
🔔 Urgency: ☐ Low ☐ Medium ☐ High		📞 Called ☐

📅 Date: **🕐 Time:**

👥 Caller:

🏢 Company:

📞 Phone:

@ Email:

🚨 Urgency: ☐ Low   ☐ Medium   ☐ High

💬 Message:

📞 Called ☐

📅 Date: **🕐 Time:**

👥 Caller:

🏢 Company:

📞 Phone:

@ Email:

🚨 Urgency: ☐ Low   ☐ Medium   ☐ High

💬 Message:

📞 Called ☐

📅 Date: **🕐 Time:**

👥 Caller:

🏢 Company:

📞 Phone:

@ Email:

🚨 Urgency: ☐ Low   ☐ Medium   ☐ High

💬 Message:

📞 Called ☐

📅 Date: **🕐 Time:**

👥 Caller:

🏢 Company:

📞 Phone:

@ Email:

🚨 Urgency: ☐ Low   ☐ Medium   ☐ High

💬 Message:

📞 Called ☐

📅 Date: **🕐 Time:**

👥 Caller:

🏢 Company:

📞 Phone:

@ Email:

🚨 Urgency: ☐ Low   ☐ Medium   ☐ High

💬 Message:

📞 Called ☐

Date: **⏰Time:**

Caller:

Company:

Phone:

Email:

Urgency: ☐ Low   ☐ Medium   ☐ High

Message:

Called ☐

Date: **⏰Time:**

Caller:

Company:

Phone:

Email:

Urgency: ☐ Low   ☐ Medium   ☐ High

Message:

Called ☐

Date: **⏰Time:**

Caller:

Company:

Phone:

Email:

Urgency: ☐ Low   ☐ Medium   ☐ High

Message:

Called ☐

Date: **⏰Time:**

Caller:

Company:

Phone:

Email:

Urgency: ☐ Low   ☐ Medium   ☐ High

Message:

Called ☐

Date: **⏰Time:**

Caller:

Company:

Phone:

Email:

Urgency: ☐ Low   ☐ Medium   ☐ High

Message:

Called ☐

📅 Date:	🕐 Time:	💬 Message:
👥 Caller:		
🏢 Company:		
📞 Phone:		
@ Email:		
🚨 Urgency: ☐ Low ☐ Medium ☐ High		📞 Called ☐

📅 Date:	🕐 Time:	💬 Message:
👥 Caller:		
🏢 Company:		
📞 Phone:		
@ Email:		
🚨 Urgency: ☐ Low ☐ Medium ☐ High		📞 Called ☐

📅 Date:	🕐 Time:	💬 Message:
👥 Caller:		
🏢 Company:		
📞 Phone:		
@ Email:		
🚨 Urgency: ☐ Low ☐ Medium ☐ High		📞 Called ☐

📅 Date:	🕐 Time:	💬 Message:
👥 Caller:		
🏢 Company:		
📞 Phone:		
@ Email:		
🚨 Urgency: ☐ Low ☐ Medium ☐ High		📞 Called ☐

📅 Date:	🕐 Time:	💬 Message:
👥 Caller:		
🏢 Company:		
📞 Phone:		
@ Email:		
🚨 Urgency: ☐ Low ☐ Medium ☐ High		📞 Called ☐

🗓 Date:	🕐 Time:	💬 Message:
👤 Caller:		
🏢 Company:		
📞 Phone:		
@ Email:		
☀ Urgency: ☐ Low ☐ Medium ☐ High		📞 Called ☐

🗓 Date:	🕐 Time:	💬 Message:
👤 Caller:		
🏢 Company:		
📞 Phone:		
@ Email:		
☀ Urgency: ☐ Low ☐ Medium ☐ High		📞 Called ☐

🗓 Date:	🕐 Time:	💬 Message:
👤 Caller:		
🏢 Company:		
📞 Phone:		
@ Email:		
☀ Urgency: ☐ Low ☐ Medium ☐ High		📞 Called ☐

🗓 Date:	🕐 Time:	💬 Message:
👤 Caller:		
🏢 Company:		
📞 Phone:		
@ Email:		
☀ Urgency: ☐ Low ☐ Medium ☐ High		📞 Called ☐

🗓 Date:	🕐 Time:	💬 Message:
👤 Caller:		
🏢 Company:		
📞 Phone:		
@ Email:		
☀ Urgency: ☐ Low ☐ Medium ☐ High		📞 Called ☐

📅 Date:	🕐 Time:	💬 Message:
👥 Caller:		
🏢 Company:		
📞 Phone:		
@ Email:		
☀ Urgency: ☐ Low ☐ Medium ☐ High		📞 Called ☐

📅 Date:	🕐 Time:	💬 Message:
👥 Caller:		
🏢 Company:		
📞 Phone:		
@ Email:		
☀ Urgency: ☐ Low ☐ Medium ☐ High		📞 Called ☐

📅 Date:	🕐 Time:	💬 Message:
👥 Caller:		
🏢 Company:		
📞 Phone:		
@ Email:		
☀ Urgency: ☐ Low ☐ Medium ☐ High		📞 Called ☐

📅 Date:	🕐 Time:	💬 Message:
👥 Caller:		
🏢 Company:		
📞 Phone:		
@ Email:		
☀ Urgency: ☐ Low ☐ Medium ☐ High		📞 Called ☐

📅 Date:	🕐 Time:	💬 Message:
👥 Caller:		
🏢 Company:		
📞 Phone:		
@ Email:		
☀ Urgency: ☐ Low ☐ Medium ☐ High		📞 Called ☐

Entry 1

Date: **Time:**

Caller:

Company:

Phone:

Email:

Urgency: ☐ Low   ☐ Medium   ☐ High

Message:

Called ☐

Entry 2

Date: **Time:**

Caller:

Company:

Phone:

Email:

Urgency: ☐ Low   ☐ Medium   ☐ High

Message:

Called ☐

Entry 3

Date: **Time:**

Caller:

Company:

Phone:

Email:

Urgency: ☐ Low   ☐ Medium   ☐ High

Message:

Called ☐

Entry 4

Date: **Time:**

Caller:

Company:

Phone:

Email:

Urgency: ☐ Low   ☐ Medium   ☐ High

Message:

Called ☐

Entry 5

Date: **Time:**

Caller:

Company:

Phone:

Email:

Urgency: ☐ Low   ☐ Medium   ☐ High

Message:

Called ☐

📅 Date:	🕐 Time:	💬 Message:
👥 Caller:		
🏢 Company:		
📞 Phone:		
@ Email:		
🚨 Urgency: ☐ Low ☐ Medium ☐ High		📞 Called ☐

📅 Date:	🕐 Time:	💬 Message:
👥 Caller:		
🏢 Company:		
📞 Phone:		
@ Email:		
🚨 Urgency: ☐ Low ☐ Medium ☐ High		📞 Called ☐

📅 Date:	🕐 Time:	💬 Message:
👥 Caller:		
🏢 Company:		
📞 Phone:		
@ Email:		
🚨 Urgency: ☐ Low ☐ Medium ☐ High		📞 Called ☐

📅 Date:	🕐 Time:	💬 Message:
👥 Caller:		
🏢 Company:		
📞 Phone:		
@ Email:		
🚨 Urgency: ☐ Low ☐ Medium ☐ High		📞 Called ☐

📅 Date:	🕐 Time:	💬 Message:
👥 Caller:		
🏢 Company:		
📞 Phone:		
@ Email:		
🚨 Urgency: ☐ Low ☐ Medium ☐ High		📞 Called ☐

Date: **Time:**   **Message:**

Caller:

Company:

Phone:

Email:

Urgency: ☐ Low   ☐ Medium   ☐ High   **Called** ☐

Date: **Time:**   **Message:**

Caller:

Company:

Phone:

Email:

Urgency: ☐ Low   ☐ Medium   ☐ High   **Called** ☐

Date: **Time:**   **Message:**

Caller:

Company:

Phone:

Email:

Urgency: ☐ Low   ☐ Medium   ☐ High   **Called** ☐

Date: **Time:**   **Message:**

Caller:

Company:

Phone:

Email:

Urgency: ☐ Low   ☐ Medium   ☐ High   **Called** ☐

Date: **Time:**   **Message:**

Caller:

Company:

Phone:

Email:

Urgency: ☐ Low   ☐ Medium   ☐ High   **Called** ☐

📅 Date:	🕐 Time:	💬 Message:
👤 Caller:		
🏢 Company:		
📞 Phone:		
@ Email:		
🚨 Urgency: ☐ Low ☐ Medium ☐ High		📞 Called ☐

📅 Date:	🕐 Time:	💬 Message:
👤 Caller:		
🏢 Company:		
📞 Phone:		
@ Email:		
🚨 Urgency: ☐ Low ☐ Medium ☐ High		📞 Called ☐

📅 Date:	🕐 Time:	💬 Message:
👤 Caller:		
🏢 Company:		
📞 Phone:		
@ Email:		
🚨 Urgency: ☐ Low ☐ Medium ☐ High		📞 Called ☐

📅 Date:	🕐 Time:	💬 Message:
👤 Caller:		
🏢 Company:		
📞 Phone:		
@ Email:		
🚨 Urgency: ☐ Low ☐ Medium ☐ High		📞 Called ☐

📅 Date:	🕐 Time:	💬 Message:
👤 Caller:		
🏢 Company:		
📞 Phone:		
@ Email:		
🚨 Urgency: ☐ Low ☐ Medium ☐ High		📞 Called ☐

Date: | **Time:** | **Message:**

Caller:

Company:

Phone:

Email:

Urgency: ☐ Low ☐ Medium ☐ High | **Called** ☐

Date: | **Time:** | **Message:**

Caller:

Company:

Phone:

Email:

Urgency: ☐ Low ☐ Medium ☐ High | **Called** ☐

Date: | **Time:** | **Message:**

Caller:

Company:

Phone:

Email:

Urgency: ☐ Low ☐ Medium ☐ High | **Called** ☐

Date: | **Time:** | **Message:**

Caller:

Company:

Phone:

Email:

Urgency: ☐ Low ☐ Medium ☐ High | **Called** ☐

Date: | **Time:** | **Message:**

Caller:

Company:

Phone:

Email:

Urgency: ☐ Low ☐ Medium ☐ High | **Called** ☐

🗓 Date:	🕐 Time:	💬 Message:
👥 Caller:		
🏢 Company:		
📞 Phone:		
@ Email:		
🚨 Urgency: ☐ Low ☐ Medium ☐ High		📞 Called ☐

🗓 Date:	🕐 Time:	💬 Message:
👥 Caller:		
🏢 Company:		
📞 Phone:		
@ Email:		
🚨 Urgency: ☐ Low ☐ Medium ☐ High		📞 Called ☐

🗓 Date:	🕐 Time:	💬 Message:
👥 Caller:		
🏢 Company:		
📞 Phone:		
@ Email:		
🚨 Urgency: ☐ Low ☐ Medium ☐ High		📞 Called ☐

🗓 Date:	🕐 Time:	💬 Message:
👥 Caller:		
🏢 Company:		
📞 Phone:		
@ Email:		
🚨 Urgency: ☐ Low ☐ Medium ☐ High		📞 Called ☐

🗓 Date:	🕐 Time:	💬 Message:
👥 Caller:		
🏢 Company:		
📞 Phone:		
@ Email:		
🚨 Urgency: ☐ Low ☐ Medium ☐ High		📞 Called ☐

Date: ⏱ Time:

👤 Caller:

🏢 Company:

📞 Phone:

@ Email:

☀ Urgency: ☐ Low   ☐ Medium   ☐ High

💬 Message:

📞 Called ☐

Date: ⏱ Time:

👤 Caller:

🏢 Company:

📞 Phone:

@ Email:

☀ Urgency: ☐ Low   ☐ Medium   ☐ High

💬 Message:

📞 Called ☐

Date: ⏱ Time:

👤 Caller:

🏢 Company:

📞 Phone:

@ Email:

☀ Urgency: ☐ Low   ☐ Medium   ☐ High

💬 Message:

📞 Called ☐

Date: ⏱ Time:

👤 Caller:

🏢 Company:

📞 Phone:

@ Email:

☀ Urgency: ☐ Low   ☐ Medium   ☐ High

💬 Message:

📞 Called ☐

Date: ⏱ Time:

👤 Caller:

🏢 Company:

📞 Phone:

@ Email:

☀ Urgency: ☐ Low   ☐ Medium   ☐ High

💬 Message:

📞 Called ☐

📅 Date:	🕐 Time:	💬 Message:
👥 Caller:		
🏢 Company:		
📞 Phone:		
@ Email:		
☀ Urgency: ☐ Low ☐ Medium ☐ High		📞 Called ☐

📅 Date:	🕐 Time:	💬 Message:
👥 Caller:		
🏢 Company:		
📞 Phone:		
@ Email:		
☀ Urgency: ☐ Low ☐ Medium ☐ High		📞 Called ☐

📅 Date:	🕐 Time:	💬 Message:
👥 Caller:		
🏢 Company:		
📞 Phone:		
@ Email:		
☀ Urgency: ☐ Low ☐ Medium ☐ High		📞 Called ☐

📅 Date:	🕐 Time:	💬 Message:
👥 Caller:		
🏢 Company:		
📞 Phone:		
@ Email:		
☀ Urgency: ☐ Low ☐ Medium ☐ High		📞 Called ☐

📅 Date:	🕐 Time:	💬 Message:
👥 Caller:		
🏢 Company:		
📞 Phone:		
@ Email:		
☀ Urgency: ☐ Low ☐ Medium ☐ High		📞 Called ☐

📅 Date:	⏰ Time:	💬 Message:
📞 Caller:		
🏢 Company:		
📞 Phone:		
@ Email:		
🔥 Urgency: ☐ Low ☐ Medium ☐ High		📞 Called ☐

📅 Date:	⏰ Time:	💬 Message:
📞 Caller:		
🏢 Company:		
📞 Phone:		
@ Email:		
🔥 Urgency: ☐ Low ☐ Medium ☐ High		📞 Called ☐

📅 Date:	⏰ Time:	💬 Message:
📞 Caller:		
🏢 Company:		
📞 Phone:		
@ Email:		
🔥 Urgency: ☐ Low ☐ Medium ☐ High		📞 Called ☐

📅 Date:	⏰ Time:	💬 Message:
📞 Caller:		
🏢 Company:		
📞 Phone:		
@ Email:		
🔥 Urgency: ☐ Low ☐ Medium ☐ High		📞 Called ☐

📅 Date:	⏰ Time:	💬 Message:
📞 Caller:		
🏢 Company:		
📞 Phone:		
@ Email:		
🔥 Urgency: ☐ Low ☐ Medium ☐ High		📞 Called ☐

🗓 Date:	⏱ Time:	💬 Message:
👤 Caller:		
🏢 Company:		
📞 Phone:		
@ Email:		
🔆 Urgency: ☐ Low ☐ Medium ☐ High		📞 Called ☐

🗓 Date:	⏱ Time:	💬 Message:
👤 Caller:		
🏢 Company:		
📞 Phone:		
@ Email:		
🔆 Urgency: ☐ Low ☐ Medium ☐ High		📞 Called ☐

🗓 Date:	⏱ Time:	💬 Message:
👤 Caller:		
🏢 Company:		
📞 Phone:		
@ Email:		
🔆 Urgency: ☐ Low ☐ Medium ☐ High		📞 Called ☐

🗓 Date:	⏱ Time:	💬 Message:
👤 Caller:		
🏢 Company:		
📞 Phone:		
@ Email:		
🔆 Urgency: ☐ Low ☐ Medium ☐ High		📞 Called ☐

🗓 Date:	⏱ Time:	💬 Message:
👤 Caller:		
🏢 Company:		
📞 Phone:		
@ Email:		
🔆 Urgency: ☐ Low ☐ Medium ☐ High		📞 Called ☐

Date: **Time:**

Message:

Caller:

Company:

Phone:

Email:

Urgency: ☐ Low ☐ Medium ☐ High   **Called** ☐

Date: **Time:**

Message:

Caller:

Company:

Phone:

Email:

Urgency: ☐ Low ☐ Medium ☐ High   **Called** ☐

Date: **Time:**

Message:

Caller:

Company:

Phone:

Email:

Urgency: ☐ Low ☐ Medium ☐ High   **Called** ☐

Date: **Time:**

Message:

Caller:

Company:

Phone:

Email:

Urgency: ☐ Low ☐ Medium ☐ High   **Called** ☐

Date: **Time:**

Message:

Caller:

Company:

Phone:

Email:

Urgency: ☐ Low ☐ Medium ☐ High   **Called** ☐

📅 Date:	🕐 Time:	💬 Message:
👥 Caller:		
🏢 Company:		
📞 Phone:		
@ Email:		
🔅 Urgency: ☐ Low ☐ Medium ☐ High		📞 Called ☐

📅 Date:	🕐 Time:	💬 Message:
👥 Caller:		
🏢 Company:		
📞 Phone:		
@ Email:		
🔅 Urgency: ☐ Low ☐ Medium ☐ High		📞 Called ☐

📅 Date:	🕐 Time:	💬 Message:
👥 Caller:		
🏢 Company:		
📞 Phone:		
@ Email:		
🔅 Urgency: ☐ Low ☐ Medium ☐ High		📞 Called ☐

📅 Date:	🕐 Time:	💬 Message:
👥 Caller:		
🏢 Company:		
📞 Phone:		
@ Email:		
🔅 Urgency: ☐ Low ☐ Medium ☐ High		📞 Called ☐

📅 Date:	🕐 Time:	💬 Message:
👥 Caller:		
🏢 Company:		
📞 Phone:		
@ Email:		
🔅 Urgency: ☐ Low ☐ Medium ☐ High		📞 Called ☐

📅 Date: _____ **🕐 Time:** _____

👤 Caller: _____

🏢 Company: _____

📞 Phone: _____

@ Email: _____

🚨 Urgency: ☐ Low ☐ Medium ☐ High

💬 Message: _____

📞 Called ☐

📅 Date: _____ **🕐 Time:** _____

👤 Caller: _____

🏢 Company: _____

📞 Phone: _____

@ Email: _____

🚨 Urgency: ☐ Low ☐ Medium ☐ High

💬 Message: _____

📞 Called ☐

📅 Date: _____ **🕐 Time:** _____

👤 Caller: _____

🏢 Company: _____

📞 Phone: _____

@ Email: _____

🚨 Urgency: ☐ Low ☐ Medium ☐ High

💬 Message: _____

📞 Called ☐

📅 Date: _____ **🕐 Time:** _____

👤 Caller: _____

🏢 Company: _____

📞 Phone: _____

@ Email: _____

🚨 Urgency: ☐ Low ☐ Medium ☐ High

💬 Message: _____

📞 Called ☐

📅 Date: _____ **🕐 Time:** _____

👤 Caller: _____

🏢 Company: _____

📞 Phone: _____

@ Email: _____

🚨 Urgency: ☐ Low ☐ Medium ☐ High

💬 Message: _____

📞 Called ☐

📅 Date:	🕐 Time:	💬 Message:
👥 Caller:		
🏢 Company:		
📞 Phone:		
@ Email:		
🚨 Urgency: ☐ Low ☐ Medium ☐ High		📞 Called ☐

📅 Date:	🕐 Time:	💬 Message:
👥 Caller:		
🏢 Company:		
📞 Phone:		
@ Email:		
🚨 Urgency: ☐ Low ☐ Medium ☐ High		📞 Called ☐

📅 Date:	🕐 Time:	💬 Message:
👥 Caller:		
🏢 Company:		
📞 Phone:		
@ Email:		
🚨 Urgency: ☐ Low ☐ Medium ☐ High		📞 Called ☐

📅 Date:	🕐 Time:	💬 Message:
👥 Caller:		
🏢 Company:		
📞 Phone:		
@ Email:		
🚨 Urgency: ☐ Low ☐ Medium ☐ High		📞 Called ☐

📅 Date:	🕐 Time:	💬 Message:
👥 Caller:		
🏢 Company:		
📞 Phone:		
@ Email:		
🚨 Urgency: ☐ Low ☐ Medium ☐ High		📞 Called ☐

▦ Date: 🕐 Time:

👤 Caller:

🏢 Company:

📞 Phone:

@ Email:

🚨 Urgency: ☐ Low   ☐ Medium   ☐ High

💬 Message:

📞 Called ☐

▦ Date: 🕐 Time:

👤 Caller:

🏢 Company:

📞 Phone:

@ Email:

🚨 Urgency: ☐ Low   ☐ Medium   ☐ High

💬 Message:

📞 Called ☐

▦ Date: 🕐 Time:

👤 Caller:

🏢 Company:

📞 Phone:

@ Email:

🚨 Urgency: ☐ Low   ☐ Medium   ☐ High

💬 Message:

📞 Called ☐

▦ Date: 🕐 Time:

👤 Caller:

🏢 Company:

📞 Phone:

@ Email:

🚨 Urgency: ☐ Low   ☐ Medium   ☐ High

💬 Message:

📞 Called ☐

▦ Date: 🕐 Time:

👤 Caller:

🏢 Company:

📞 Phone:

@ Email:

🚨 Urgency: ☐ Low   ☐ Medium   ☐ High

💬 Message:

📞 Called ☐

📇 Date:	🕐 Time:	💬 Message:
👥 Caller:		
🏢 Company:		
📞 Phone:		
@ Email:		
🔆 Urgency: ☐ Low ☐ Medium ☐ High		📞 Called ☐

📇 Date:	🕐 Time:	💬 Message:
👥 Caller:		
🏢 Company:		
📞 Phone:		
@ Email:		
🔆 Urgency: ☐ Low ☐ Medium ☐ High		📞 Called ☐

📇 Date:	🕐 Time:	💬 Message:
👥 Caller:		
🏢 Company:		
📞 Phone:		
@ Email:		
🔆 Urgency: ☐ Low ☐ Medium ☐ High		📞 Called ☐

📇 Date:	🕐 Time:	💬 Message:
👥 Caller:		
🏢 Company:		
📞 Phone:		
@ Email:		
🔆 Urgency: ☐ Low ☐ Medium ☐ High		📞 Called ☐

📇 Date:	🕐 Time:	💬 Message:
👥 Caller:		
🏢 Company:		
📞 Phone:		
@ Email:		
🔆 Urgency: ☐ Low ☐ Medium ☐ High		📞 Called ☐

Date: **Time:**   **Message:**

Caller:

Company:

Phone:

Email:

Urgency: ☐ Low   ☐ Medium   ☐ High   **Called** ☐

Date: **Time:**   **Message:**

Caller:

Company:

Phone:

Email:

Urgency: ☐ Low   ☐ Medium   ☐ High   **Called** ☐

Date: **Time:**   **Message:**

Caller:

Company:

Phone:

Email:

Urgency: ☐ Low   ☐ Medium   ☐ High   **Called** ☐

Date: **Time:**   **Message:**

Caller:

Company:

Phone:

Email:

Urgency: ☐ Low   ☐ Medium   ☐ High   **Called** ☐

Date: **Time:**   **Message:**

Caller:

Company:

Phone:

Email:

Urgency: ☐ Low   ☐ Medium   ☐ High   **Called** ☐

📅 Date:	🕐 Time:	💬 Message:
👤 Caller:		
🏢 Company:		
📞 Phone:		
@ Email:		
☼ Urgency: ☐ Low ☐ Medium ☐ High		📞 Called ☐

📅 Date:	🕐 Time:	💬 Message:
👤 Caller:		
🏢 Company:		
📞 Phone:		
@ Email:		
☼ Urgency: ☐ Low ☐ Medium ☐ High		📞 Called ☐

📅 Date:	🕐 Time:	💬 Message:
👤 Caller:		
🏢 Company:		
📞 Phone:		
@ Email:		
☼ Urgency: ☐ Low ☐ Medium ☐ High		📞 Called ☐

📅 Date:	🕐 Time:	💬 Message:
👤 Caller:		
🏢 Company:		
📞 Phone:		
@ Email:		
☼ Urgency: ☐ Low ☐ Medium ☐ High		📞 Called ☐

📅 Date:	🕐 Time:	💬 Message:
👤 Caller:		
🏢 Company:		
📞 Phone:		
@ Email:		
☼ Urgency: ☐ Low ☐ Medium ☐ High		📞 Called ☐

Date:	Time:	Message:
Caller:		
Company:		
Phone:		
Email:		
Urgency: ☐ Low ☐ Medium ☐ High		Called ☐

Date:	Time:	Message:
Caller:		
Company:		
Phone:		
Email:		
Urgency: ☐ Low ☐ Medium ☐ High		Called ☐

Date:	Time:	Message:
Caller:		
Company:		
Phone:		
Email:		
Urgency: ☐ Low ☐ Medium ☐ High		Called ☐

Date:	Time:	Message:
Caller:		
Company:		
Phone:		
Email:		
Urgency: ☐ Low ☐ Medium ☐ High		Called ☐

Date:	Time:	Message:
Caller:		
Company:		
Phone:		
Email:		
Urgency: ☐ Low ☐ Medium ☐ High		Called ☐

🖩 Date:	🕐 Time:	💬 Message:
👤 Caller:		
🏛 Company:		
📞 Phone:		
@ Email:		
🔆 Urgency: ☐ Low ☐ Medium ☐ High		📞 Called ☐

🖩 Date:	🕐 Time:	💬 Message:
👤 Caller:		
🏛 Company:		
📞 Phone:		
@ Email:		
🔆 Urgency: ☐ Low ☐ Medium ☐ High		📞 Called ☐

🖩 Date:	🕐 Time:	💬 Message:
👤 Caller:		
🏛 Company:		
📞 Phone:		
@ Email:		
🔆 Urgency: ☐ Low ☐ Medium ☐ High		📞 Called ☐

🖩 Date:	🕐 Time:	💬 Message:
👤 Caller:		
🏛 Company:		
📞 Phone:		
@ Email:		
🔆 Urgency: ☐ Low ☐ Medium ☐ High		📞 Called ☐

🖩 Date:	🕐 Time:	💬 Message:
👤 Caller:		
🏛 Company:		
📞 Phone:		
@ Email:		
🔆 Urgency: ☐ Low ☐ Medium ☐ High		📞 Called ☐

📅 Date: _____ **🕐 Time:** _____

👤 Caller: _____

🏢 Company: _____

📞 Phone: _____

@ Email: _____

🔔 Urgency: ☐ Low ☐ Medium ☐ High

💬 Message: _____

📞 Called ☐

📅 Date: _____ **🕐 Time:** _____

👤 Caller: _____

🏢 Company: _____

📞 Phone: _____

@ Email: _____

🔔 Urgency: ☐ Low ☐ Medium ☐ High

💬 Message: _____

📞 Called ☐

📅 Date: _____ **🕐 Time:** _____

👤 Caller: _____

🏢 Company: _____

📞 Phone: _____

@ Email: _____

🔔 Urgency: ☐ Low ☐ Medium ☐ High

💬 Message: _____

📞 Called ☐

📅 Date: _____ **🕐 Time:** _____

👤 Caller: _____

🏢 Company: _____

📞 Phone: _____

@ Email: _____

🔔 Urgency: ☐ Low ☐ Medium ☐ High

💬 Message: _____

📞 Called ☐

📅 Date: _____ **🕐 Time:** _____

👤 Caller: _____

🏢 Company: _____

📞 Phone: _____

@ Email: _____

🔔 Urgency: ☐ Low ☐ Medium ☐ High

💬 Message: _____

📞 Called ☐

📅 Date:	🕐 Time:	💬 Message:
👥 Caller:		
🏢 Company:		
📞 Phone:		
@ Email:		
🔆 Urgency: ☐ Low ☐ Medium ☐ High		📞 Called ☐

📅 Date:	🕐 Time:	💬 Message:
👥 Caller:		
🏢 Company:		
📞 Phone:		
@ Email:		
🔆 Urgency: ☐ Low ☐ Medium ☐ High		📞 Called ☐

📅 Date:	🕐 Time:	💬 Message:
👥 Caller:		
🏢 Company:		
📞 Phone:		
@ Email:		
🔆 Urgency: ☐ Low ☐ Medium ☐ High		📞 Called ☐

📅 Date:	🕐 Time:	💬 Message:
👥 Caller:		
🏢 Company:		
📞 Phone:		
@ Email:		
🔆 Urgency: ☐ Low ☐ Medium ☐ High		📞 Called ☐

📅 Date:	🕐 Time:	💬 Message:
👥 Caller:		
🏢 Company:		
📞 Phone:		
@ Email:		
🔆 Urgency: ☐ Low ☐ Medium ☐ High		📞 Called ☐

📅 Date: _____ **🕐 Time:** _____ | **💬 Message:**

👤 Caller: _____

🏛 Company: _____

📞 Phone: _____

@ Email: _____

☀ Urgency: ☐ Low ☐ Medium ☐ High | **📞 Called ☐**

📅 Date: _____ **🕐 Time:** _____ | **💬 Message:**

👤 Caller: _____

🏛 Company: _____

📞 Phone: _____

@ Email: _____

☀ Urgency: ☐ Low ☐ Medium ☐ High | **📞 Called ☐**

📅 Date: _____ **🕐 Time:** _____ | **💬 Message:**

👤 Caller: _____

🏛 Company: _____

📞 Phone: _____

@ Email: _____

☀ Urgency: ☐ Low ☐ Medium ☐ High | **📞 Called ☐**

📅 Date: _____ **🕐 Time:** _____ | **💬 Message:**

👤 Caller: _____

🏛 Company: _____

📞 Phone: _____

@ Email: _____

☀ Urgency: ☐ Low ☐ Medium ☐ High | **📞 Called ☐**

📅 Date: _____ **🕐 Time:** _____ | **💬 Message:**

👤 Caller: _____

🏛 Company: _____

📞 Phone: _____

@ Email: _____

☀ Urgency: ☐ Low ☐ Medium ☐ High | **📞 Called ☐**

📅 Date:	🕐 Time:	💬 Message:
👥 Caller:		
🏛 Company:		
🕐 Phone:		
@ Email:		
🔆 Urgency: ☐ Low ☐ Medium ☐ High		📞 Called ☐

📅 Date:	🕐 Time:	💬 Message:
👥 Caller:		
🏛 Company:		
🕐 Phone:		
@ Email:		
🔆 Urgency: ☐ Low ☐ Medium ☐ High		📞 Called ☐

📅 Date:	🕐 Time:	💬 Message:
👥 Caller:		
🏛 Company:		
🕐 Phone:		
@ Email:		
🔆 Urgency: ☐ Low ☐ Medium ☐ High		📞 Called ☐

📅 Date:	🕐 Time:	💬 Message:
👥 Caller:		
🏛 Company:		
🕐 Phone:		
@ Email:		
🔆 Urgency: ☐ Low ☐ Medium ☐ High		📞 Called ☐

📅 Date:	🕐 Time:	💬 Message:
👥 Caller:		
🏛 Company:		
🕐 Phone:		
@ Email:		
🔆 Urgency: ☐ Low ☐ Medium ☐ High		📞 Called ☐

Date:	Time:	Message:
Caller:		
Company:		
Phone:		
Email:		
Urgency: ☐ Low ☐ Medium ☐ High		Called ☐

Date:	Time:	Message:
Caller:		
Company:		
Phone:		
Email:		
Urgency: ☐ Low ☐ Medium ☐ High		Called ☐

Date:	Time:	Message:
Caller:		
Company:		
Phone:		
Email:		
Urgency: ☐ Low ☐ Medium ☐ High		Called ☐

Date:	Time:	Message:
Caller:		
Company:		
Phone:		
Email:		
Urgency: ☐ Low ☐ Medium ☐ High		Called ☐

Date:	Time:	Message:
Caller:		
Company:		
Phone:		
Email:		
Urgency: ☐ Low ☐ Medium ☐ High		Called ☐

📅 Date:	🕐 Time:	💬 Message:
👥 Caller:		
🏢 Company:		
📞 Phone:		
@ Email:		
🔆 Urgency: ☐ Low ☐ Medium ☐ High		📞 Called ☐

📅 Date:	🕐 Time:	💬 Message:
👥 Caller:		
🏢 Company:		
📞 Phone:		
@ Email:		
🔆 Urgency: ☐ Low ☐ Medium ☐ High		📞 Called ☐

📅 Date:	🕐 Time:	💬 Message:
👥 Caller:		
🏢 Company:		
📞 Phone:		
@ Email:		
🔆 Urgency: ☐ Low ☐ Medium ☐ High		📞 Called ☐

📅 Date:	🕐 Time:	💬 Message:
👥 Caller:		
🏢 Company:		
📞 Phone:		
@ Email:		
🔆 Urgency: ☐ Low ☐ Medium ☐ High		📞 Called ☐

📅 Date:	🕐 Time:	💬 Message:
👥 Caller:		
🏢 Company:		
📞 Phone:		
@ Email:		
🔆 Urgency: ☐ Low ☐ Medium ☐ High		📞 Called ☐

Date: **Time:** | **Message:**
Caller:
Company:
Phone:
Email:
Urgency: ☐ Low ☐ Medium ☐ High | **Called** ☐

Date: **Time:** | **Message:**
Caller:
Company:
Phone:
Email:
Urgency: ☐ Low ☐ Medium ☐ High | **Called** ☐

Date: **Time:** | **Message:**
Caller:
Company:
Phone:
Email:
Urgency: ☐ Low ☐ Medium ☐ High | **Called** ☐

Date: **Time:** | **Message:**
Caller:
Company:
Phone:
Email:
Urgency: ☐ Low ☐ Medium ☐ High | **Called** ☐

Date: **Time:** | **Message:**
Caller:
Company:
Phone:
Email:
Urgency: ☐ Low ☐ Medium ☐ High | **Called** ☐

🗓 Date:	⏱ Time:	💬 Message:
👥 Caller:		
🏢 Company:		
📞 Phone:		
@ Email:		
🚨 Urgency: ☐ Low ☐ Medium ☐ High		📞 Called ☐

🗓 Date:	⏱ Time:	💬 Message:
👥 Caller:		
🏢 Company:		
📞 Phone:		
@ Email:		
🚨 Urgency: ☐ Low ☐ Medium ☐ High		📞 Called ☐

🗓 Date:	⏱ Time:	💬 Message:
👥 Caller:		
🏢 Company:		
📞 Phone:		
@ Email:		
🚨 Urgency: ☐ Low ☐ Medium ☐ High		📞 Called ☐

🗓 Date:	⏱ Time:	💬 Message:
👥 Caller:		
🏢 Company:		
📞 Phone:		
@ Email:		
🚨 Urgency: ☐ Low ☐ Medium ☐ High		📞 Called ☐

🗓 Date:	⏱ Time:	💬 Message:
👥 Caller:		
🏢 Company:		
📞 Phone:		
@ Email:		
🚨 Urgency: ☐ Low ☐ Medium ☐ High		📞 Called ☐

Date: 📅 **Time:** 🕑 **Message:** 💬

Caller: 👤

Company: 🏢

Phone: 📞

Email: @

Urgency: 🚨 ☐ Low ☐ Medium ☐ High   **Called** ☎ ☐

Date: 📅 **Time:** 🕑 **Message:** 💬

Caller: 👤

Company: 🏢

Phone: 📞

Email: @

Urgency: 🚨 ☐ Low ☐ Medium ☐ High   **Called** ☎ ☐

Date: 📅 **Time:** 🕑 **Message:** 💬

Caller: 👤

Company: 🏢

Phone: 📞

Email: @

Urgency: 🚨 ☐ Low ☐ Medium ☐ High   **Called** ☎ ☐

Date: 📅 **Time:** 🕑 **Message:** 💬

Caller: 👤

Company: 🏢

Phone: 📞

Email: @

Urgency: 🚨 ☐ Low ☐ Medium ☐ High   **Called** ☎ ☐

Date: 📅 **Time:** 🕑 **Message:** 💬

Caller: 👤

Company: 🏢

Phone: 📞

Email: @

Urgency: 🚨 ☐ Low ☐ Medium ☐ High   **Called** ☎ ☐

📅 Date:	🕐 Time:	💬 Message:
👤 Caller:		
🏢 Company:		
📞 Phone:		
@ Email:		
☀ Urgency: ☐ Low ☐ Medium ☐ High		📞 Called ☐

📅 Date:	🕐 Time:	💬 Message:
👤 Caller:		
🏢 Company:		
📞 Phone:		
@ Email:		
☀ Urgency: ☐ Low ☐ Medium ☐ High		📞 Called ☐

📅 Date:	🕐 Time:	💬 Message:
👤 Caller:		
🏢 Company:		
📞 Phone:		
@ Email:		
☀ Urgency: ☐ Low ☐ Medium ☐ High		📞 Called ☐

📅 Date:	🕐 Time:	💬 Message:
👤 Caller:		
🏢 Company:		
📞 Phone:		
@ Email:		
☀ Urgency: ☐ Low ☐ Medium ☐ High		📞 Called ☐

📅 Date:	🕐 Time:	💬 Message:
👤 Caller:		
🏢 Company:		
📞 Phone:		
@ Email:		
☀ Urgency: ☐ Low ☐ Medium ☐ High		📞 Called ☐

🗓 Date:	⏱ Time:	💬 Message:
👤 Caller:		
🏛 Company:		
📞 Phone:		
@ Email:		
☼ Urgency: □ Low □ Medium □ High		📞 Called □

🗓 Date:	⏱ Time:	💬 Message:
👤 Caller:		
🏛 Company:		
📞 Phone:		
@ Email:		
☼ Urgency: □ Low □ Medium □ High		📞 Called □

🗓 Date:	⏱ Time:	💬 Message:
👤 Caller:		
🏛 Company:		
📞 Phone:		
@ Email:		
☼ Urgency: □ Low □ Medium □ High		📞 Called □

🗓 Date:	⏱ Time:	💬 Message:
👤 Caller:		
🏛 Company:		
📞 Phone:		
@ Email:		
☼ Urgency: □ Low □ Medium □ High		📞 Called □

🗓 Date:	⏱ Time:	💬 Message:
👤 Caller:		
🏛 Company:		
📞 Phone:		
@ Email:		
☼ Urgency: □ Low □ Medium □ High		📞 Called □

Date:	Time:	Message:
Caller:		
Company:		
Phone:		
@ Email:		
Urgency: ☐Low ☐Medium ☐High		Called ☐

Date:	Time:	Message:
Caller:		
Company:		
Phone:		
@ Email:		
Urgency: ☐Low ☐Medium ☐High		Called ☐

Date:	Time:	Message:
Caller:		
Company:		
Phone:		
@ Email:		
Urgency: ☐Low ☐Medium ☐High		Called ☐

Date:	Time:	Message:
Caller:		
Company:		
Phone:		
@ Email:		
Urgency: ☐Low ☐Medium ☐High		Called ☐

Date:	Time:	Message:
Caller:		
Company:		
Phone:		
@ Email:		
Urgency: ☐Low ☐Medium ☐High		Called ☐

Made in the USA
Monee, IL
25 April 2024

57473489R00061